Excel®
Macros & VBA
For Business Users
A Beginners Guide

C.J. Benton

ISBN-10: 1530946549
ISBN-13: 978-1530946549

DEDICATION

For business users searching for a practical
Microsoft® Macros and VBA book!

Other Books Available From This Author:

1. Microsoft® Excel® **Start Here** The Beginners Guide

2. The Step-By-Step Guide To The **25 Most Common** Microsoft® Excel® Formulas & Features

3. The Step-By-Step Guide To **Pivot Tables &** Introduction To **Dashboards**

4. The Step-By-Step Guide To The **VLOOKUP** formula in Microsoft® Excel®

5. The Microsoft® Excel® Step-By-Step Training Guide **Book Bundle**

Table of Contents

CHAPTER 1 1

How To Use This Book 1

CHAPTER 2 6

An Introduction To Macros & VBA (Visual Basic for Applications) 6

What is a Macro? 6

What is VBA (Visual Basic for Applications)?..............................7

What is the Excel® Object Model?...7

Sub-Procedure 7

Function-Procedure 7

Object 8

Properties 8

Method 8

Variables 9

CHAPTER 3 13

The Developer Tab 13

Record Macro 14

Macro Security..15

Macros 17

Absolute vs. Relative Reference Macro Recording...................17

Visual Basic 20

CHAPTER 4 21

Recording your first macro & the VBA Editor 21

Recording your first macro – *part 1* 21

Testing the macro...24

The VBA Editor..25

Saving a macro file...27

Recording your first macro – *part 2* 29

How to insert comments in your macro....................................32

How to add additional code to an existing macro....................35

Testing the macro...36

Modifying code in an existing macro...37

Renaming an existing macro..39

Deleting a macro...41

CHAPTER 5..43
The Personal Macro Workbook & Macro buttons................43
   What is the Personal Macro Workbook?.......................43
   Adding a macro button to the 'Quick Access Toolbar' 49
CHAPTER 6..51
Recording a relative reference macro - example for ad hoc reporting 51
   MACRO OBJECTIVES 51
   STEPS TO RECORD MACRO.......................................53
   CODE REVIEW 55
   UNDERSTANDING R1C1 CELL RANGES 56
CHAPTER 7..60
How to use the 'Debug' tools 60
   Program Errors 60
   Logic Errors 63
   Controlled Error Messages 68
CHAPTER 8..70
Report macro #1 – recording a macro to format a monthly report......70
   MACRO OBJECTIVES 70
   STEPS TO RECORD MACRO.......................................71
   CODE REVIEW 74
CHAPTER 9..77
Data Analysis Macro – analyzing test results.......................77
   MACRO OBJECTIVES 77
   STEPS TO RECORD MACRO.......................................79
   CODE REVIEW 83
CHAPTER 10..86
Using macros and Pivot Tables to parse text or .CSV files 86
   MACRO OBJECTIVES (file type = text)..........................86
   STEPS TO RECORD MACRO (text file – part #1)..............88
   CODE REVIEW 93
   STEPS TO RECORD MACRO (text file – part #2)..............95
   Adding a macro button (controls) 97
   PIVOT TABLE OBJECTIVES (file type = .CSV)..................99
   STEPS TO CREATE PIVOT TABLE (.CSV file) 101
CHAPTER 11..110
Introduction To Loop Structures....................................110
   For Each...Next Loop...112
   Do...Loop 113
   Conceptual diagram of Do...Loop types 113
   STEPS TO CREATE MACRO 115
   CODE REVIEW 117

CHAPTER 12 120
How to use IF...THEN...ELSE and Select...Case Statements in macros . 120
   STEPS TO CREATE MACRO (Basic IF...THEN...ELSE) 121
   CODE REVIEW (Basic IF...THEN...ELSE) 123
   STEPS TO CREATE MACRO (If...Then...ElseIf...Else) 124
   STEPS TO CREATE MACRO (Select...Case) 126
   CODE REVIEW (Select...Case) 128
CHAPTER 13 129
Data Analysis Macro #2 – Enhanced comparative analysis 129
   MACRO OBJECTIVES 129
   STEPS TO CREATE MACRO 131
   CODE REVIEW 132
CHAPTER 14 136
Report macro #2 – Dynamic Quarterly & Year-To-Date reporting 136
   MACRO OBJECTIVES 136
   STEPS TO CREATE MACRO 138
   CODE REVIEW 139
CHAPTER 15 143
Macro to print all worksheets in a workbook 143
   MACRO OBJECTIVES 143
   STEPS TO CREATE MACRO 143
CHAPTER 16 146
Macro to save each worksheet as a separate workbook files 146
   MACRO OBJECTIVES 146
   STEPS TO CREATE MACRO 146
CHAPTER 17 149
Macros to sort worksheets either alphabetically or numerically 149
   MACRO OBJECTIVES 149
   STEPS TO CREATE MACRO 150
CHAPTER 18 154
Protecting macro code 154
Appendix A 156
Document Inspector 156
A MESSAGE FROM THE AUTHOR 158

PREFACE

For nearly twenty years, I worked as a Data & Systems Analyst for three different Fortune 500 companies, primarily in the areas of Finance, Infrastructure Services, and Logistics. During that time I used Microsoft® Excel® extensively, developing hundreds of different types of reports, analysis tools, and several forms of Dashboards.

I've utilized many Microsoft® Excel® formulas & features, the following are the basic skills and knowledge all users should have when using macros.

CHAPTER 1
How To Use This Book

This book can be used as a tutorial or quick reference guide and was written for **non-programmers**. Intended specifically for business users, such as Business Analysts, Data Analysts, Administrative staff, Quality Assurance Analysts, and Support personnel who are proficient with the basics of Microsoft® Excel® and are now ready to improve their skills further by learning about macros and VBA (**V**isual **B**asic for **A**pplications).

This book assumes you already know how to create, open, save, and modify an Excel® workbook, including cutting and pasting. Have a general understanding of formulas and familiarity with the Excel® toolbar (Ribbon).

All of the examples in this book use Microsoft® Excel® 2013, however most of the functionality can be applied with Microsoft® Excel® version 2007 or later with some minor modifications.

While this book provides several basic, intermediate, and advanced macro examples, it does not cover ALL available Microsoft® Excel® VBA and macro functionality.

Please always **back-up your work** and **save often**. A good best practice when attempting any new functionality is to **create a copy of the original spreadsheet** and implement your changes on the copied spreadsheet. Should anything go wrong, you then have the original spreadsheet to fall back on. Please see the diagram below.

Diagram 1:

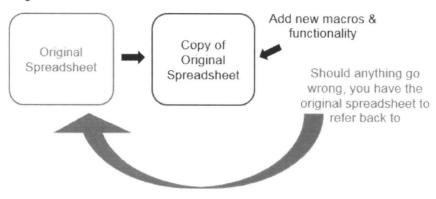

The book is divided into five segments, it begins by providing a foundation on how macros work, followed by step-by-step examples of recording and troubleshooting macros. Continuing with how to enhance your code with Looping and Decision Structures, and concludes with how macros can be applied to improve productivity.

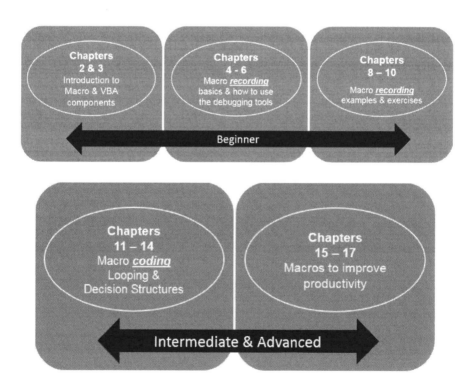

To assist with readability and to give the examples more business context, the macro exercise chapters consist of one or more of the following sections:

Diagram 2:

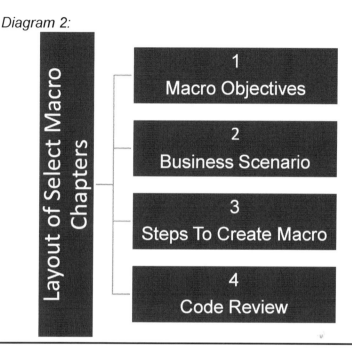

SECTION 1:
Outlines the specific functionality demonstrated in the exercise.

SECTION 2:
Describes a business scenario representing how the macro may be applied.

SECTION 3:
Explains how to develop the macro to resolve the chapter's business scenario.

SECTION 4:
Provides a detailed explanation with screenshots on how the macro code works.

FILES FOR EXERCISES

The file name and website path to download the exercise file is located within each applicable chapter.

Each exercise file consists of:

1. One or more worksheets to apply the macro
2. One or more worksheets with the macro code that may copied and pasted into a module (*Modules are explained in the next chapter*).

EXAMPLE:

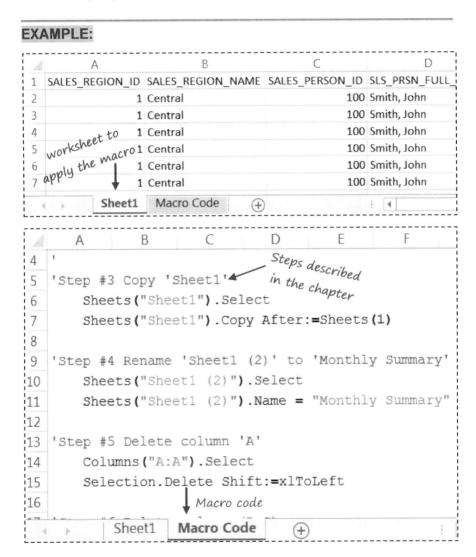

Occasionally when saving Excel® macro files you'll receive the following message:

Be careful! Parts of your document may include personal information that can't be removed by the Document Inspector.

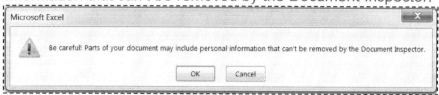

This is caused because Microsoft® does not support the automatic removal of hidden information for documents that use Information Rights Management (IRM).

You may click the **'OK'** button to bypass the message or follow the instructions outlined in <u>Appendix A</u> to launch the **'Document Inspector'** feature within Excel® to inspect the document

CHAPTER 2

An Introduction To Macros & VBA (Visual Basic for Applications)

What is a Macro?

An Excel® macro automates a set of actions within one or more workbooks. An action can be a keystroke or spreadsheet command.

Any steps you do repeatedly in Excel®, such as formatting reports, dynamically creating invoices, analyzing data, updating inventory records, or parsing and importing files, can often be automated with a macro.

Macros are frequently created by *recording* a user's actions on a specific spreadsheet. However, macros can also be developed by someone who has basic programming skills or technical aptitude to piece together code snippets to automate a particular task.

Macros may be referred to as programs, procedures, scripts, or even applications. Macros, when called, can perform sophisticated tasks very quickly; saving time, improving workflow, and reducing the chance of errors to standardized processes.

While some macros are modest in their application and may not require you to review or edit the code, such as macros that format cells, insert text, or apply basic formulas. Others are more complex and require structured planning, organization, development, and testing. These type of macros may include importing data from other applications, looping through records, calling other workbooks, or applying User-Defined Functions (UDFs).

What is VBA (Visual Basic for Applications)?

VBA (**V**isual **B**asic for **A**pplications) is the programming language used to develop a macro in Microsoft® Excel®. VBA code instructs a macro to complete a series of actions on one or more spreadsheets based on the VBA code *recorded* or *written*.

VBA is not limited to Excel®, the programming language is available in other Microsoft® Office® products such as Word® and PowerPoint®. This book focuses on using VBA to create macros in Excel®.

What is the Excel® Object Model?

When you record or write a macro, VBA calls this a *module*. There are two types of VBA modules, a *sub-procedure* and *function-procedure.*

Sub-Procedure

1) Sub-procedures are primarily what non-programmers use because many of these types of macros can be recorded and perform multiple actions on one or more *objects (see next page for the term 'object's' definition).*

> For example, a sub-procedure macro may be recorded to select cells **'A1: D1'** and change the format of the font to bold.

Function-Procedure

2) Function-procedures need to be written in VBA code, typically involve some type of calculation, and return a single value.

> Functions may sound familiar to you, as Excel® already provides built-in functions. Some examples include *sum, min, max,* and *count.*

Object

Objects are things that can be changed, such as a workbook, worksheet, or cell. Microsoft® Excel® refers to these objects in a *hierarchy* called the ***Excel® Object Model***.

When you record or write a macro you're **transforming one or more Excel® objects**.

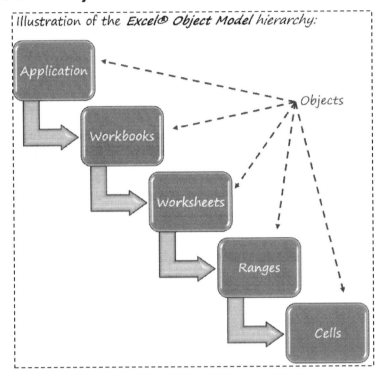

Each object has *properties* and *methods* associated with them.

Properties

Properties are often referred to as **attributes,** because they describe a piece of information about the object such as formatting or visibility.

Method

A **Method** refers to an action that can be performed on that object, such as *select* or *value*.

In the example below, this sub-procedure (macro) selects cell A1 and changes the font format to bold:

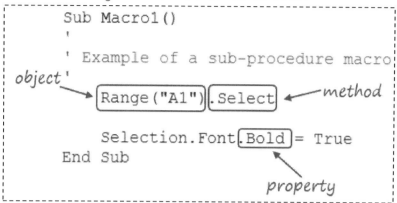

Another part of either a *sub-procedure* or *function-procedure* is called a *variable*.

Variables

Variables are temporary holders of information, such as text or numeric data. You'll be able to record many macros without declaring variables. However, to leverage more advanced macro functionality, such as looping, dynamic reporting, worksheet sorting etc. you'll at least want to know variables exist and how to edit them if necessary.

When should you use a macro?

Macros improve productivity and reduce the chance of errors occurring when you have to repeat the same steps over and over. They are ideal for **automating** many tasks such as:

   ✓ The **formatting** of reports, invoices, and forms. Any time you have to repeat adding titles, inserting formulas, columns, rows, changing font styles, etc.

✓ The **dissemination of information** that must be separated by customer, division, region, department etc.

✓ The **preparation of spreadsheets** for analysis, testing, or to be imported by another application or database.

✓ When repeating actions on an **ad hoc report**, such as formulas and formatting.

When are macros not worth the investment?

Since some macros require planning, development, and testing they are not useful for:

- **Short-term assignments:** For example, if testing for a given project requires less than ten iterations, the effort to build and test a macro may not be worth the time.

- **Limited Technical Support**: For instance, when you're developing a macro for a customer or colleague, but will not be able to support it.

   If something goes wrong and there are no other resources that can be cross-trained to provide assistance, careful consideration should be given to any macro development.

   While the macro would be providing a solution to a repetitive task, a process would be implemented that could not be sustained.

However, sometimes these risks can't be avoided, they are outweighed by the value the macro brings to process efficiency and accuracy.

Macro limitations

As much as I like how macros make my life and my fellow colleagues lives easier, they do have their limitations. The biggest short-comings being:

- **No automatic undo functionality**. With most Microsoft® Office® products, we've become very accustom to being able to undo our actions. However, with macros we lose this benefit.

- **No record at mark feature.** For some reason Microsoft® does not allow you to *record* additional tasks to an existing macro. Therefore, appending or modifying existing macros is more time consuming.

The unintended consequences of automation:

As your experience with macros grows, you'll see more and more opportunities to utilize them, however your process improvement efforts may not always be welcome. Some users like to be in control and do not like it when a set of tasks is performed "behind the scenes". If your organization has an IT (**I**nformation **T**echnology) department, they may disapprove of you, as a business user automating or developing programs. This usually stems from the IT department being unable to respond to the needs of the business in a timely manner.

I've worked for both business and IT departments, I've had to support many Excel® / macro spreadsheets that were intended to be *"temporary fixes"* until IT could provide a permanent solution. However, these short-term workarounds (some quite elaborate) became part of production processes for months or even years.

Be mindful of this and test your macros regularly. If the macros you develop are being used for any type of customer facing, government, or regulatory compliance, take the extra time to plan, test thoroughly, and document your work. You don't want to risk credibility with your customers or superiors for producing low quality, inaccurate, or overly complicated systems.

The biggest pitfalls a business user takes when developing macros is a failure to test properly and the inability to support or maintain the macro as needed. Similarly, if you're automating a job function that someone did manually, it is possible for them to feel threatened by this and believe their job is potentially being jeopardized by your macros. It is important to be sensitive to this and attempt to identify areas where your macro enables them to spend more time on responsibilities that cannot be automated.

Also, depending on the person and their willingness to learn, you could cross-train them on the macro you developed. Teaching them how to record and troubleshoot basic macros provides them with a valuable new skill, gives them more control, and empowers, rather than takes away a value they use to provide.

CHAPTER 3
The Developer Tab

Before recording our first macro, we need to activate the **'Developer'**
tab on the Microsoft® Excel® Ribbon.

If the **'Developer'** tab is not active, from the **'File'** tab select:
1. Options
2. Customize Ribbon
3. Click the '**Developer**' check box
4. Click the '**OK**' button

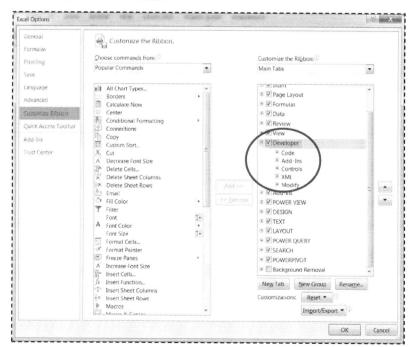

Once added, you'll find the Developer tab contains five sections:
1. Code
2. Add-Ins
3. Controls
4. XML
5. Document Panel (Modify)

This book focus on the **'Code'** section of the 'Developer' tab. As your technical experience with macros grows you may eventually have a need to use XML, the COM (**C**omponent **O**bject **M**odel), or Automation Add-ins, however the **'Code'** segment contains the functionality utilized the most, by the majority of business users.

Description of the 'Code' functionality of the 'Developer' tab:

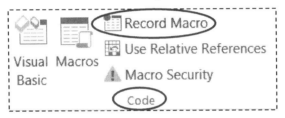

Record Macro

The next chapter goes into detail on recording macros, however a brief description of the **'Record Macro'** option is when you want to begin recording a macro, you would click the **'Record Macro'** field

Record Macro. You would then be prompted to give the macro a name. Once you click the **'OK'** button, from name prompt, any tasks you perform will be recorded and the **'Stop Recording'** button will become active.

Macro Security

To set the macro security for the version of Excel® installed on your computer, click the 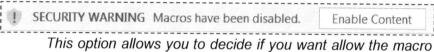 ⚠ Macro Security field. The following dialogue box will appear with four macro security options:

1. **Disable all macros without notification:** This option prevents any macros from running. The highest level of macro security.

2. **Disable all macros with notification**: Macros are disabled, but you'll be prompted with the below security message if the file contains a macro.

> ❗ SECURITY WARNING Macros have been disabled.   Enable Content

    This option allows you to decide if you want allow the macro to run on a file-by-file basis.

3. **Disable all macros except digitally signed macros:** This is similar to option #2, except if the macro is digitally signed by a trusted publisher, the macro will run if you have *"trusted"* the publisher.

4. **Enable all macros (not recommended, potentially dangerous code can run)**: **Do not** use this setting, this option will leave your computer susceptible to malicious programs.

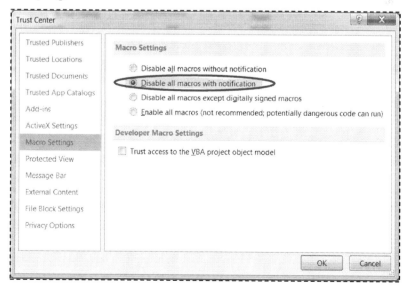

The setting most often recommended, is the second option *'Disable all macros with notification'*.

Please note, if you develop a macro for someone else, they too will need to enable / allow permission to run a macro in their version of Excel®.

This is also the first area to check when a user says *"your macro doesn't work"*. However, they do not need to activate the 'Developer' tab to access the above menu. You can always access the 'Trust Center' in Excel®, by selecting **File → Options → Trust Center** and clicking the **'Trust Center Settings'** button as shown below:

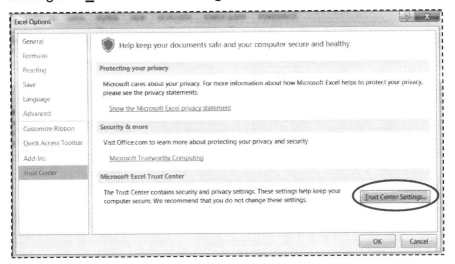

Select **'Macro Settings'** from the menu:

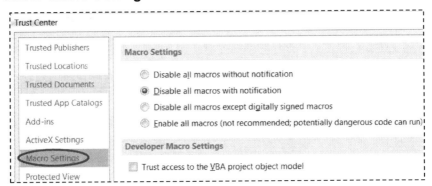

Macros

When clicked, the **'Macro'** button will launch a dialogue box and display the available macros to run from any open workbook.

Absolute vs. Relative Reference Macro Recording

Most of the macros you develop will use **absolute references.** This means each time your macro runs, it will perform the recorded or coded action, on the specific cell or cells you have identified.

For example, you recorded a macro that formats cell **'A2'** of the active worksheet to be bold. Each time you run this macro, cell **'A2'** of the active worksheet will be formatted in bold. **'A2'** in this example, is **absolute**. Another way to think about absolute recording is **'A2'** is being held constant $A$2 (the reference is absolute).

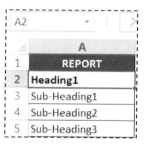

Now let's say you're working on an **ad hoc report** and want to format each heading to be bold and each sub-heading to be aligned right.

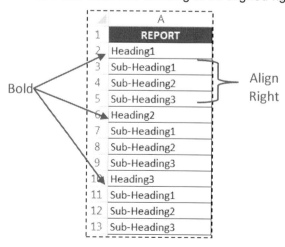

Depending on the size of your report, it may be quicker to record an macro with **relative references.**

Excel® gives you the option to record a macro using **relative references.** When the 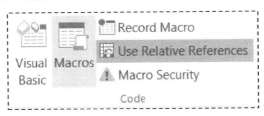 field of the 'Code' section of the **'Developer' tab** is highlighted *before* clicking the **'Record Macro'** field.

When a relative macro runs, it will perform the coded action, on a cell or cells *depending on where it is launched. The cells are not specific (absolute).*

In the example below, the macro with relative references would **bold** the active cell and **indent the following three cells**, regardless of where it is launched.

If you placed your cursor in cell **'A6'**, and ran the macro with relative references, it would bold cell **'A6'** and indent cells **'A7: A9'**.

It would repeat this action if you launched on cell **'A10'**. The macro would bold cell **'A10'** and indent cells **'A11 : A13'**.

	A
1	**REPORT**
2	**Heading1**
3	Sub-Heading1
4	Sub-Heading2
5	Sub-Heading3
6	**Heading2**
7	Sub-Heading1
8	Sub-Heading2
9	Sub-Heading3
10	**Heading3**
11	Sub-Heading1
12	Sub-Heading2
13	Sub-Heading3

Similarly, since this relative reference macro is bolding the active cell and indenting the following three cells, if you launched on cell '**A13**', the following unintended formatting would occur:

	A
1	**REPORT**
2	**Heading1**
3	Sub-Heading1
4	Sub-Heading2
5	Sub-Heading3
6	**Heading2**
7	Sub-Heading1
8	Sub-Heading2
9	Sub-Heading3
10	**Heading3**
11	Sub-Heading1
12	Sub-Heading2
13	**Sub-Heading3**
14	Heading4
15	Sub-Heading1
16	Sub-Heading2
17	Sub-Heading3

Unintended formatting

You're likely already familiar with relative references. When you copy and paste a formula and do not hold the cells constant, this is an example of using **relative references**.

*Examples of **relative reference** formulas:*

	A	B	C
1	1	3	5
2	2	4	6
3	=SUM(A1:A2)	=SUM(B1:B2)	=SUM(C1:C2)

Examples of **absolute reference** formulas:

	A	B	C
1	1	3	5
2	2	4	6
3	=SUM($A$1:$A$2)	=SUM($B$1:$B$2)	=SUM($C$1:$C$2)

Visual Basic
When clicked, the **'Visual Basic'** field will launch the *VBA Editor*. The next chapter reviews this editor in detail.

CHAPTER 4

Recording your first macro & the VBA Editor

MACRO OBJECTIVES:

In the following exercise, (recording your first macro – part 1) we will review:

1. How to record a macro
2. How to test a macro
3. How to open the VBA Editor
4. Saving a macro file with the .**xlsm** extension

Recording your first macro – ***part 1***

1. Create a new blank Excel® spreadsheet **(CTRL + N)**

2. Add the following text and numbers to cells **'A1:C4'**:

▲	A	B	C
1	STORE	APPLES	ORANGES
2	AAA	200.00	150.00
3	BBB	300.00	250.00
4	CCC	400.00	350.00

3. **Save** the file, you may want to name it something like:
   - Chapter04_RecordingYourFirstMacro.xlsx

4. Select the '**Developer**' tab and verify the '**Use Relative References**' field is **NOT highlighted**:

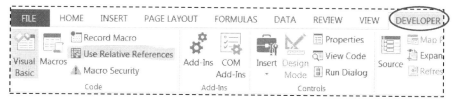

5. Place your cursor in cell '**E1**' and click the '**Record Macro**' field:

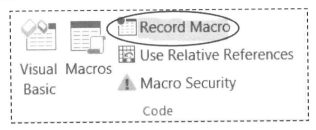

The following dialogue box will appear:

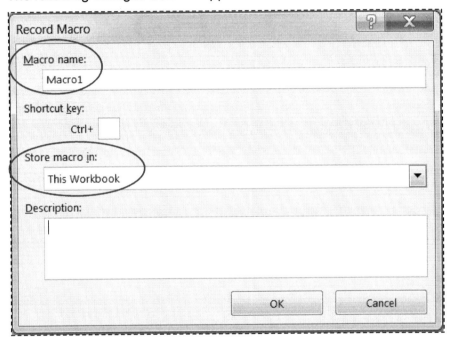

6. Enter '**Bold_Row1**' in the '**Macro name:**' field

7. Verify the '**Store macro in:**' has '**This Workbook**' selected in the drop-down box

8. Click the '**OK**' button

A few notes about naming a macro:

When you name a macro, you're naming a *sub-procedure* or *function-procedure*. When *recording* this will always be a *sub-procedure*. The following rules apply to naming both types of procedures:

    a)   The only special character you can use is the underscore (_)
    b)   You can't use spaces in the name

---

9.   Bold cells '**A1:C1**'

10. From the '**DEVELOPER**' tab click the '**Stop Recording**' field

I realize changing the format of three cells is not very exciting, the objective in part 1 is to familiarize yourself with the macro recording process and the VBA Editor. As we progress the exercises will become more challenging.

Testing the macro

1. Un-bold cells '**A1:C1**'

2. Select the '**Developer**' tab and click the '**Macros**' field:

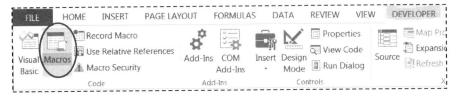

The following dialogue box will appear:

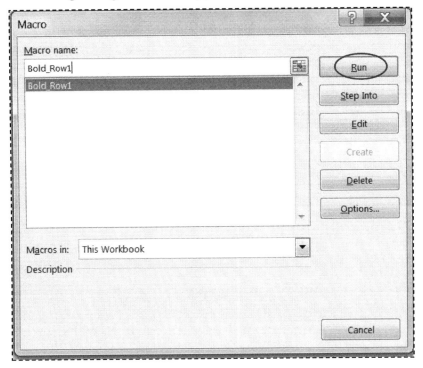

3. Verify the '**Macros in:**' drop-down box has '**This Workbook**' selected

4. Select '**Bold_Row1**' macro

5. Click the '**Run**' button

Cells '**A1:C1**' should now be bold

The VBA Editor

Why in a book written for business users do we need to have basic understanding of how the VBA editor works? For three main reasons:

1. Even with basic formatting macros, you'll still want to add *comments* to the code. This is extremely helpful for yourself and others who may support the macro at a later date.

2. **Troubleshooting**, you'll eventually need to know how to step through the code to address errors. This is also known as debugging.

3. **Modifying macros**, such as copying, pasting, deleting, and commenting out sections of code. This will be particularly useful when appending to existing macros.

To view the VBA code for the macro we just recorded:
1. Select the '**Developer**' tab and click the '**Macros**' field

The following dialogue box will appear:

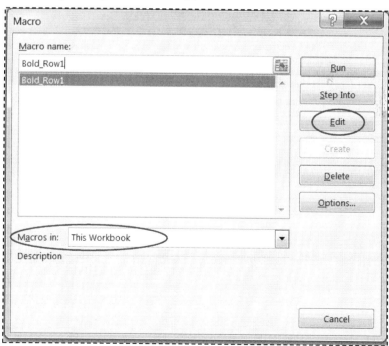

2. Verify the '**Macros in:**' drop-down box has '**This Workbook**' selected

3. Select '**Bold_Row1**' macro

4. Click the '**Edit**' button

The VBA Editor should open and look *similar* to the following:

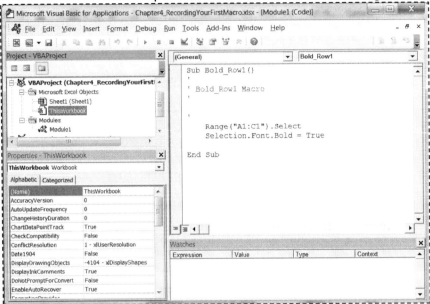

Examining a few sections of the VBA Editor:

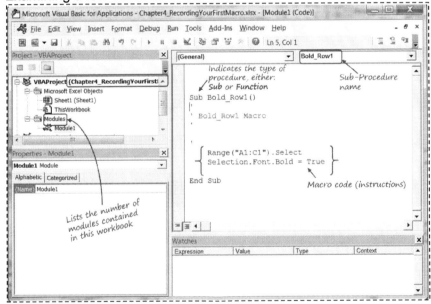

We'll be examining the **VBA Editor** more in part 2 of this chapter.

Saving a macro file

Saving a macro file is slightly different than how you would normally save an Excel® workbook. Excel® workbooks with macros associated with them must be saved with the **.xlsm** extension instead of **.xlsx**. Let's walk-through an example:

1. Un-bold cells '**A1:C1**'

2. Click the '**Save**' button or (**CTRL+S**) on the file that has the '**Bold_Row1**' macro:
   '*Chapter04_RecordingYourFirstMacro.xlsx*'

3. If you receive the following prompt, click the '**No**' button

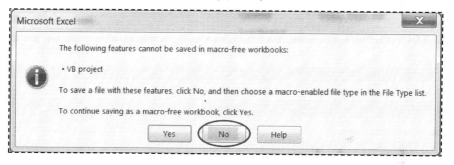

4. When prompted, click the drop-down box '**Save as type:**'

5. Select the option '**Excel Macro-Enabled Workbook (*xlsm)**

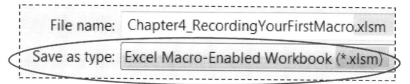

6. Click the '**Save**' button

7. Close and reopen the file, you'll notice the different icons between a **.xlsm** and **.xlsx** workbook.

When you reopen the file, depending on your security settings you may receive the following prompt:

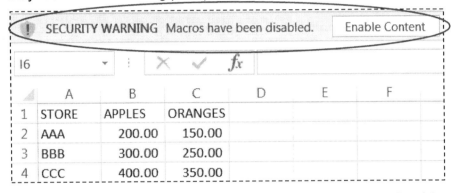

Since you know this macro is safe, go ahead and click the '**Enable Content**' button. We'll be using this file again in the next section.

MACRO OBJECTIVES:

In the following exercise, (recording your first macro – *part 2*) we will review:

1. How to insert comments in your macro
2. How to add additional code to an existing macro
3. How to comment out sections of code
4. How to modify code in an existing macro
5. Renaming a macro
6. Deleting a macro

Recording your first macro – *part 2*

Once you have a macro developed, you may identify an enhancement; or a change in the business process may requires a change to the macro. Unfortunately, this not as easy as I think it should be. Microsoft® does not allow you to **record additional tasks** to an existing macro. This leaves us with three options:

1. Start over - scrap the existing macro and record a new one with the enhancements or required modifications.

2. Manually change or add the additional code to the existing module (macro).

3. Record a separate new macro with the improvements or alterations and manually copy and paste this new code into the existing macro.

Depending on your situation, you may decide starting over is the best choice. Especially, if your macro is not very long, complicated, and does not require a lot of testing.

If you're familiar with the VBA programming language, manually changing or adding code to the existing module (macro) may be an option.

One of the most common ways to improve or make changes to your existing macro is to record a separate new macro with the improvements or alterations, and manually copy and paste this new code into the existing macro. Let's walk through an example.

1. If not already open, please open the macro file we just created: '*Chapter04_RecordingYourFirstMacro.xlsm*'

2. In cell **'D1'** add the word **'MANGOS'**

3. In cell **'D2'** add the number **'100.00'**

4. In cell **'D3'** add the number **'200.00'**

5. In cell **'D4'** add the number **'325.00'**

Your spreadsheet should look similar to the following:

	A	B	C	D
1	STORE	APPLES	ORANGES	MANGOS
2	AAA	200.00	150.00	100.00
3	BBB	300.00	250.00	200.00
4	CCC	400.00	350.00	325.00

6. Select the '**Developer**' tab and verify the '**Use Relative References**' field is **NOT highlighted**

7. Place your cursor in cell '**E1**' and click the '**Record Macro**' field:

8. Enter '**Format_NumbersToCurrency**' in the '**Macro name:**' field

9. Verify the '**Store macro in:**' has '**This Workbook**' selected in the drop-down box

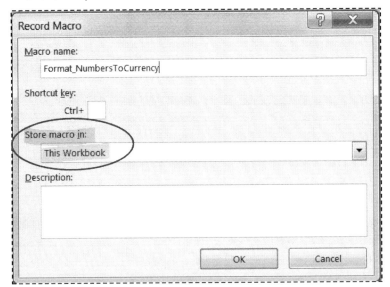

10. Click the '**OK**' button

11. Change cells '**B2:D4**' to a currency of your choice

12. Reduce the decimal places to zero

For this example, I will use the British Pound £

13. Select cell '**E1**'

14. Click the '**Stop Recording**' field

15. Select the '**Developer**' tab, click the **'Visual Basic'** field

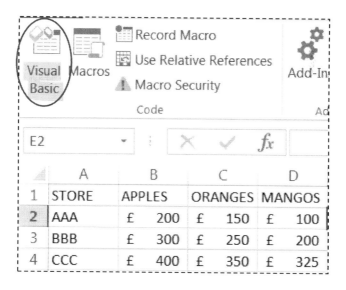

The VBA Editor should open and look *similar* to the following:

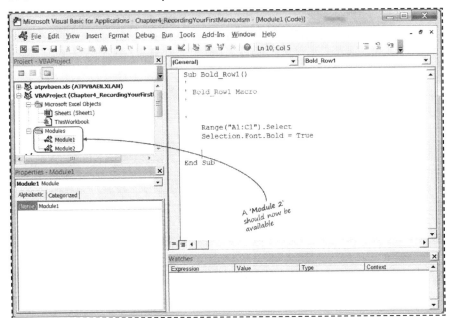

How to insert comments in your macro

Comments are a great way to add information about who or what department, when, and why a macro was developed. The comments can be brief. For example, you may want to add something like the following :

```
'Developed by Sales Department 06 Feb 2016
'Analyst <name>
'To standardize the formatting of monthly reports
```

This type of information is especially helpful if any problems occur at a later date with the macro. Even if the person who originally developed the macro has left you can contact their replacement or have some idea who to go to with questions.

1. In **Module1** place your cursor under the line:
    ```
    Sub Bold_Row1( )
    ```

2. Type a single quote and the following text (**comments**), you'll notice the font turns green after your cursor leaves the active line.

```
'Developed by Sales Department 06 Feb 2016
'Analyst <name>
'To standardize the formatting of monthly reports
```

3. In **Module1** place your cursor under the existing code:

```
Range("A1:C1").Select
Selection.Font.Bold = True
```

4. Type a single quote and the following text (**comments**):

```
'Inserting additional currency formatting
'This section of code was added on 06-02-2016
```

A macro will pass over any line of code with a single quote inserted in front of it, allowing us to add informative comments.

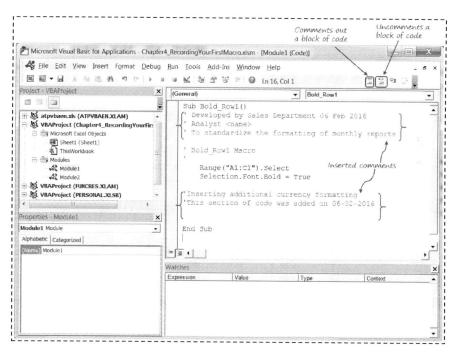

You may also add '**Comment / Uncomment block**' commands to your toolbar.

   A. Right click on the toolbar

   B. Select **'Customize...'**

   C. Drag the preferred **'Commands'** to the toolbar

   D. When finished click the **'Close'** button

How to add additional code to an existing macro

1. Double click **'Module2'**

A *similar* picture as the following should appear:

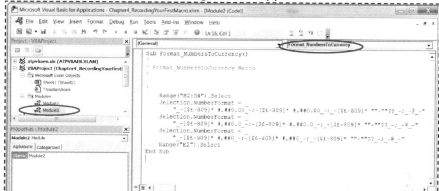

2. Highlight the code between the words:
   'Sub Format_NumbersToCurrency()' and **'End Sub'**

3. From the Ribbon select **'Edit : Copy'** or **CTRL+C**

4. Double click **'Module1'**

5. Place your cursor below the inserted comments:

```
'Inserting additional currency formatting
'This section of code was added on 06-02-2016
```

6. From the Ribbon select **'Edit : Paste'** or **CTRL+V**

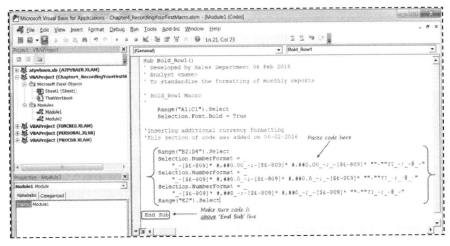

7. Save the macro, from the Ribbon select **'File : Save'** or **CTRL+S**

8. Close the VBA Editor

Testing the macro

1. Return to the *'Chapter04_RecordingYourFirstMacro.xlsm'* workbook

2. Change cells **'B2:D4'** back to the number format, with two decimal points

3. Save the *'Chapter04_RecordingYourFirstMacro.xlsm'* file **with no formatting changes**

	A	B	C	D
1	STORE	APPLES	ORANGES	MANGOS
2	AAA	200.00	150.00	100.00
3	BBB	300.00	250.00	200.00
4	CCC	400.00	350.00	325.00

4. Select the **'Developer'** tab and click the **'Macros'** field

5. When macro dialogue box appears, select the **'Bold_Row1'** macro

6. Click the **'Run'** button

You'll notice the macro did not bold cell **'D1'**, this is ok, we'll address this in the next section.

	A	B	C	D
1	**STORE**	**APPLES**	**ORANGES**	**MANGOS**
2	AAA	£ 200	£ 150	£ 100
3	BBB	£ 300	£ 250	£ 200
4	CCC	£ 400	£ 350	£ 325

7. Close the *'Chapter04_RecordingYourFirstMacro.xlsm'* file **without saving the changes**

Modifying code in an existing macro

As your experience with recording macros grows, you may eventually feel comfortable making minor adjustments to the VBA code. This is a natural progression and one that will also be helpful when troubleshooting and debugging macros. Let's walk through an example.

1. Please open the macro file we recently closed: *'**Chapter04_RecordingYourFirstMacro.xlsm**'*

The workbook should look similar to the following. If you recall the macro **'Bold_Row1'** did not bold cell **'D1'**. In following steps we're going to modify the existing code to include changing the format of cell **'D1'** to bold.

	A	B	C	D
1	STORE	APPLES	ORANGES	MANGOS
2	AAA	200.00	150.00	100.00
3	BBB	300.00	250.00	200.00
4	CCC	400.00	350.00	325.00

2. Select the 'Developer' tab, click the 'Visual Basic' field

3. Double click 'Module1' macro 'Bold_Row1'

4. Copy the line of code: `Range("A1:C1").Select`

5. Paste the copied code under the line we just copied

6. Comment out the original line of code. *This step, while not necessary ensures we always have the original code to refer back to should our modifications fail*

7. Change the new line of code to now include cell 'D1' `Range("A1:D1").Select`

8. Save the macro

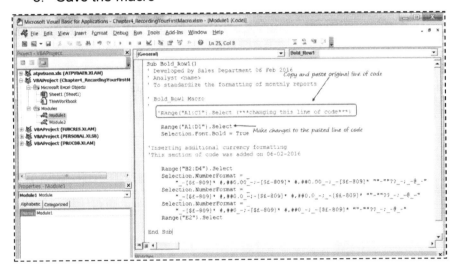

9. Test the macro

The results should look similar to the following:

	A	B	C	D
1	STORE	APPLES	ORANGES	MANGOS
2	AAA	£ 200	£ 150	£ 100
3	BBB	£ 300	£ 250	£ 200
4	CCC	£ 400	£ 350	£ 325

Once we test and verify the **'Bold_Row1'** macro is working, we can change the name to something more applicable.

Renaming an existing macro

1. If closed, please open the file:
   'Chapter04_RecordingYourFirstMacro.xlsm'

2. Select the '**Developer**' tab, click the **'Macro'** field

3. Verify the **'Store macro in:'** has **'This Workbook'** selected in the drop-down box

4. Select the **'Bold_Row1'** macro and click the **'Edit'** button

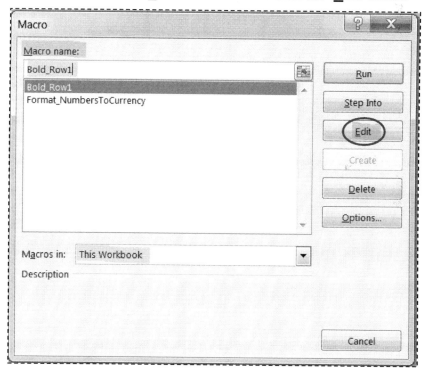

The VBA editor will open

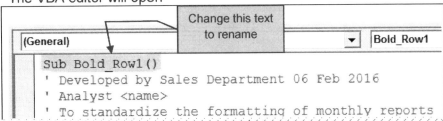

5. Rename Sub **'Bold_Row1'** to something more meaningful such as:

   ▪ FormattingMacro_Row1_Currency

6. Save the macro and file

The new name should now appear in the **'Macro'** dialogue box:

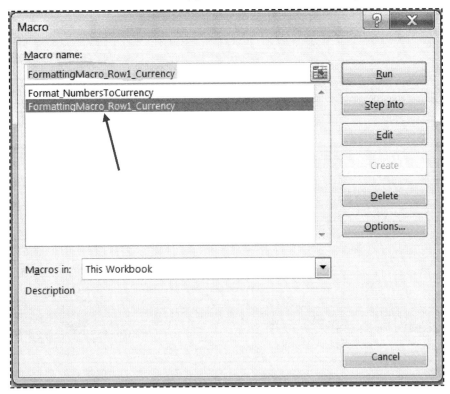

Deleting a macro

1. If closed, please open the file:
'*Chapter04_RecordingYourFirstMacro.xlsm*'

2. Select the '**Developer**' tab, click the **'Macro'** field

3. Verify the **'Store macro in:'** has **'This Workbook'** selected in the drop-down box

4. Select the **'Format_NumbersToCurrency'** macro and click the **'Delete'** button

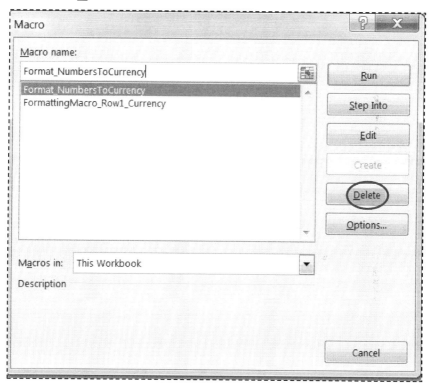

5. Click the **'Yes'** button when prompted:

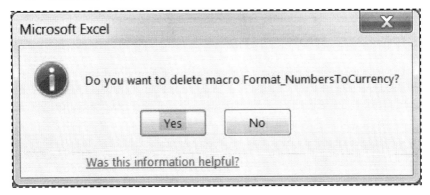

6. Save the macro and file

The **'Format_NumbersToCurrency'** macro should now be removed:

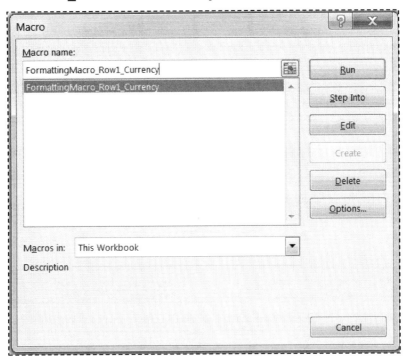

CHAPTER 5

The Personal Macro Workbook & Macro buttons

What is the Personal Macro Workbook?

The Personal Macro Workbook is a file named **'PERSONAL.XLSB'** in which you can store and access macros that you want available for all workbooks. In chapter 4, the macros we recorded were workbook specific, meaning only available when that particular workbook is open.

As you learn more about macros, you'll likely find ways to apply automated functionality across various types of workbooks. Some examples include:

- ✓ Un-hiding all hidden worksheets
- ✓ Sorting worksheet tabs in alphabetical or numeric order
- ✓ Saving files with a specific name, date, and timestamp
- ✓ Report preparation macros, such as when you receive a new file on a weekly or monthly basis
- ✓ Analysis macros you may use for project testing

And much more. With the 'PERSONAL.XLSB' macro workbook, you have access to your most frequently used macros.

Let's walk through an example, in the following steps we'll create a macro that *un-hides all hidden worksheets*.

1. Create a new blank Excel® spreadsheet **(CTRL + N)**

2. Add three to four new worksheets

3. Select the '**Developer**' tab and verify the '**Use Relative References**' field is **NOT highlighted**

4. Click the '**Record Macro**' field

When the following dialogue box appears:

5. Enter a meaningful '**Macro name:**' such as 'Unhide_All_Worksheets'

6. Add a '**Shortcut key:**' letter, in this example I'm using the letter 'y'

7. In the '**Store macro in:**' select '**Personal Macro Workbook**' from the drop-down box

8. Optionally, add a brief '**Description:**'

9. Click the '**OK**' button

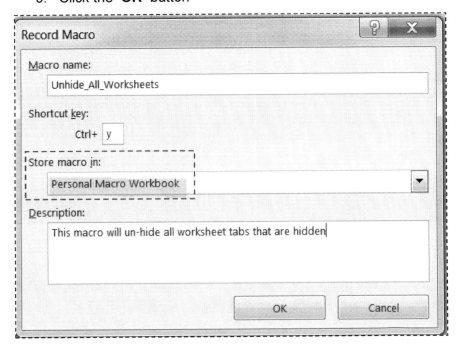

10. Click the '**Stop Recording**' field, there is nothing to record, we're going to *manually* add two lines of code for this macro

11. Click the **'Macros'** field, from the **'Developer'** tab

12. Verify the **'Macros in:'** drop-down box has the **PERSONAL.XLSB** file selected

13. At the prompt, click the **'Edit'** button for the **'Unhide_All_Worksheets'** macro or whatever you named it

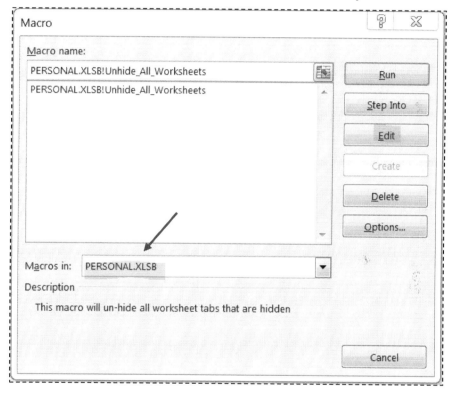

You'll receive the following message:

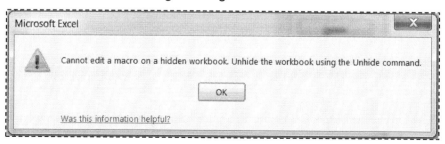

The 'PERSONAL.XLSB' macro workbook is hidden by default. To unhide:

14. From the Ribbon select **'VIEW : Unhide'**

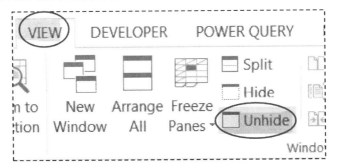

For the 'PERSONAL.XLSB' macro workbook, I added the text **'Personal Macro workbook'** to remind myself to hide this workbook before exiting.

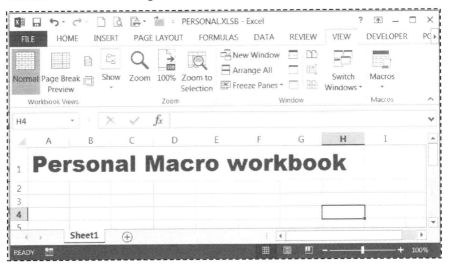

15. Select the '**Developer**' tab and click the **'Visual Basic'** field

The VBA Editor will open

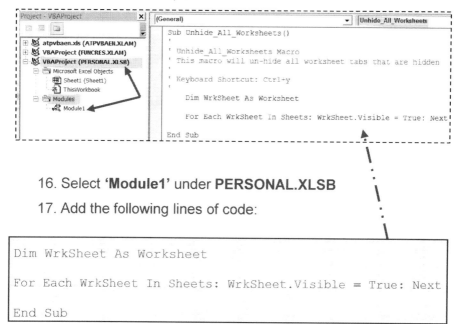

16. Select **'Module1'** under **PERSONAL.XLSB**

17. Add the following lines of code:

```
Dim WrkSheet As Worksheet

For Each WrkSheet In Sheets: WrkSheet.Visible = True: Next

End Sub
```

These lines of code are actually a 'For Each...Next' loop, the concept of looping is introduced in <u>chapter 11</u>, but the macro is appropriate for this excercise.

18. Click the **'Save'** button or **'CTRL+S'** from the **VBA Editor** to save the coding changes to the **'PERSONAL.XLSB'** macro workbook

19. **Hide** the **'PERSONAL.XLSB'** macro workbook *(from the Ribbon select 'VIEW : Hide')*

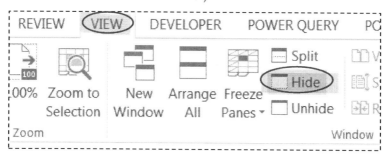

20. Test the macro by returning to the spreadsheet with the extra tabs and **hide** them

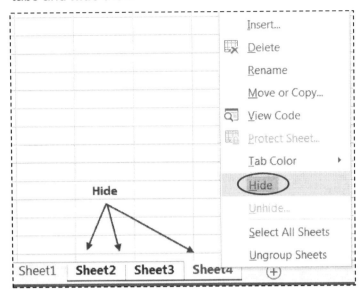

21. Press **CTRL + Y** on your keyboard _or_ from the '**Developer**' tab, click the '**Macros**' field and run the macro

All worksheets that were previously hidden should now be displayed.

When exiting Excel®, after making changes to the '**PERSONAL.XLSB**' workbook, you may be prompted with the following message:

Click '**Save**' when prompted to save changes to the '**Personal Macro Workbook**'

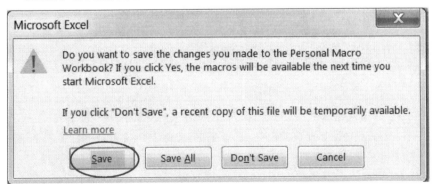

Adding a macro button to the 'Quick Access Toolbar'

To add a macro button to the '**Quick Access Toolbar**' or '**Ribbon**':

1. Access the:
   - '**Customize Quick Access Toolbar...**' *or*
   - '**Customize the Ribbon...**' prompt

*By **right clicking** on the '**Quick Access Toolbar**', I'm able to access the following menu:*

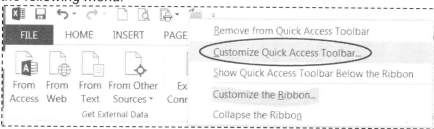

In this example, I've selected the: **Customize Quick Access**

Toolbar

2. In the '**Choose commands from:**' drop-down box, select '**Macros**'

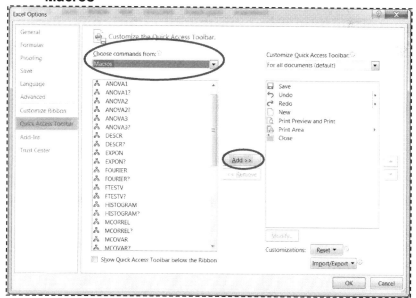

3. Select the **'PERSONAL.XLSB!Unhide_All_Worksheets'** macro from the list

4. Click the '**Add >>**' button

5. Once added you may change the symbol of the button, by clicking the **'Modify…'** button.

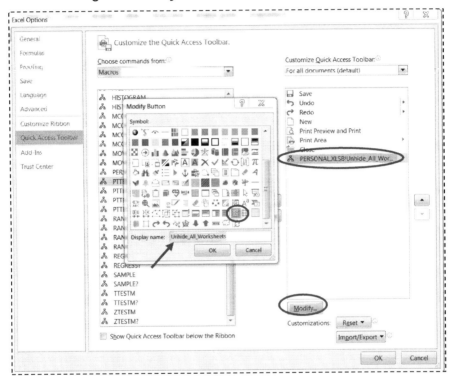

The macro button has been added the: <u>C</u>ustomize Quick Access **Toolbar**

I've found it helpful to either provide these instructions for colleagues that I've developed macros for or add the button for them as part of the macro training process.

CHAPTER 6

Recording a relative reference macro - example for ad hoc reporting

- Recording a relative reference macro for an ad hoc report
- Create shortcut key for a relative reference macro
- Review how R1C1 cell ranges work

SCENARIO:

You're a Business Analyst that supports a manufacturing company of aerospace parts. You've been asked to quickly prepare a sales report for an unplanned meeting. This report will be used only one time by divisional sales managers. Your requirements:

1. Apply formatting to easily identify each division
2. Total the number of parts sold for each division

WEB ADDRESS & FILE NAME FOR EXERCISE:
http://bentonexcelbooks.my-free.website/macro-exercise-files

Chapter06_RelativeReferenceForAdHocReporting.xlsx

C.J. Benton

EXAMPLE:
From:

	A	B
1	DIVISIONAL SALES (QTY SOLD)	
2	January 2016	
3		
4	Division - A	
5	Structural	24
6	Fuel	11
7	Power	13
8	Wing	23
9	Division - B	
10	Structural	9
11	Fuel	16
12	Power	11
13	Wing	14
14	Division - C	

To:

	A	B	C
1	DIVISIONAL SALES (QTY SOLD)		
2	January 2016		
3	Division - A		
4	Structural	24	
5	Fuel	11	
6	Power	13	
7	Wing	23	
8	TOTAL	71	
9	Division - B		
10	Structural	9	
11	Fuel	16	
12	Power	11	
13	Wing	14	
14	TOTAL	50	

STEPS TO RECORD MACRO

1. Open the file
   Chapter06_RelativeReferenceForAdHocReporting.xlsx

2. Select the '**Developer**' tab and verify the '**Use Relative References**' field *is* **highlighted**:

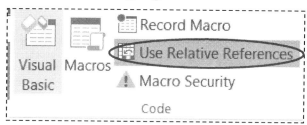

3. Place your cursor in cell '**A3**'

4. Click the '**Record Macro**' field

5. When prompted, enter a name for the macro, such as '*AdHoc_Formatting*' or something similar

6. For the '**Shortcut key:**' enter the letter '**m**'

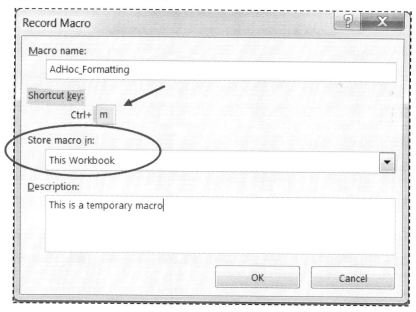

7. Bold active cell, which should be cell **'A3'**

8. Align right the following four rows, cells **'A4:A7'**

9. Insert a row after row 7

10. Insert the sum formula to cell **'B8'** `=SUM(B4:B7)` to sum the quantity of parts sold

11. Add the word **'TOTAL'** to cell **'A8'**

12. **Bold** and shade grey cells 'A8:B8'

13. Place cursor in cell **'A9'**

14. From the Ribbon select **DEVELOPER : Stop Recording**'

15. Test the macro by pressing **CTRL+M** on your keyboard

The results should be similar to the following:

	A	B	C
1	**DIVISIONAL SALES (QTY SOLD)**		
2	**January 2016**		
3	**Division - A**		
4	Structural	24	
5	Fuel	11	
6	Power	13	
7	Wing	23	
8	**TOTAL**	**71**	
9	**Division - B**		
10	Structural	9	
11	Fuel	16	
12	Power	11	
13	Wing	14	
14	**TOTAL**	**50**	
15	Division - C		

CODE REVIEW

```
(General)                                    AdHoc_Formatting

Sub AdHoc_Formatting()
'
' AdHoc_Formatting Macro
' This is a temporary macro
'
' Keyboard Shortcut: Ctrl+m
'
'Step #7 - bold active cell
    Selection.Font.Bold = True

'Step #8 - Align right the next 4 cells in column A
    ActiveCell.Offset(1, 0).Range("A1:A4").Select
    With Selection
        .HorizontalAlignment = xlRight
        .VerticalAlignment = xlBottom
        .WrapText = False
        .Orientation = 0
        .AddIndent = False
        .IndentLevel = 0
        .ShrinkToFit = False
        .ReadingOrder = xlContext
        .MergeCells = False
    End With
```

```
'Step #9 - Insert Row
    ActiveCell.Offset(4, 0).Rows("1:1").EntireRow.Select
    Selection.Insert Shift:=xlDown, CopyOrigin:=xlFormatFromLeftOrAbove

'Step #10 - Add formula to sum the quantity of parts sold
    ActiveCell.Offset(0, 1).Range("A1").Select
    ActiveCell.FormulaR1C1 = "=SUM(R[-4]C:R[-1]C)"

'Step #11 - Add the text TOTAL to the inserted line
    ActiveCell.Offset(0, -1).Range("A1").Select
    ActiveCell.FormulaR1C1 = "TOTAL"

'Step #12 - Make bold and add shading to the inserted line
    ActiveCell.Range("A1:B1").Select
    Selection.Font.Bold = True
    With Selection.Interior
        .Pattern = xlSolid
        .PatternColorIndex = xlAutomatic
        .ThemeColor = xlThemeColorDark1
        .TintAndShade = -0.149998474074526
        .PatternTintAndShade = 0
    End With

'Step #13 - Place cursor in cell for macro formatting to be repeated
    ActiveCell.Offset(1, 0).Range("A1").Select
End Sub
```

UNDERSTANDING R1C1 CELL RANGES

You may have noticed when we recorded step #10 of the above macro, *"add sum formula to cell 'B8' =SUM(B4:B7) to sum the quantity of parts sold,"* the following was recorded:

```
'Step #10 - Add formula to sum the quantity of parts sold
    ActiveCell.Offset(0, 1).Range("A1").Select
    ActiveCell.FormulaR1C1 = "=SUM(R[-4]C:R[-1]C)"
```

You may not recognize:

```
    ActiveCell.FormulaR1C1 = "=SUM(R[-4]C:R[-1]C)"
```

Similarly you may have recorded your own macros, applied a formula, and upon review, saw something similar to the following. A simple sum formula such as the one below in cell 'C3' for cells 'A3+B3' displayed as:

```
    Range("C3").Select
    ActiveCell.FormulaR1C1 = "=RC[-2]+RC[-1]"

    Range("C4").Select
    ActiveCell.FormulaR1C1 = "=SUM(RC[-2]:RC[-1])"
```

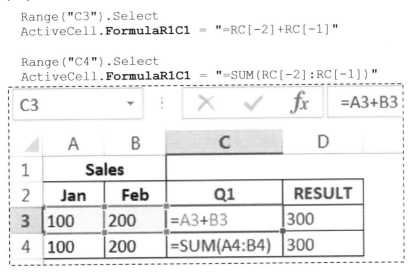

When recording macros, regardless of the 'Use Relative References' field being active, Excel® always records formulas using what is referred to as **R1C1 style**. **This should not affect how you record your macros**. I review this topic to provide a basic understanding of how formulas are recorded, to aid with troubleshooting, and to assist if you *manually modify* the code of an existing macro. Let's take a closer look at how R1C1 formula recording works.

- R1C1 is represented as **R[ ]C = Rows** and **RC[ ] = Columns**

- **RC[ ]** with a *negative* number in the bracket [ ] refers to the number of **columns left** of the cell where the formula is active.

- **RC[ ]** with a *positive* number in the bracket [ ] refers to the number of **columns right** of the cell where the formula is active.

- **R[ ]C** with a *negative* number in the bracket [ ] refers to the number of **rows up** of the cell where the formula is active.

- **R[ ]C** with a *positive* number in the bracket [ ] refers to the number of **rows below** of the cell where the formula is active.

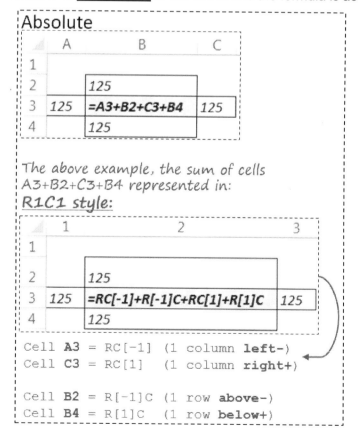

Absolute

	A	B	C
1			
2		125	
3	125	=A3+B2+C3+B4	125
4		125	

The above example, the sum of cells A3+B2+C3+B4 represented in:

R1C1 style:

	1	2	3
1			
2		125	
3	125	=RC[-1]+R[-1]C+RC[1]+R[1]C	125
4		125	

```
Cell A3 = RC[-1]  (1 column left-)
Cell C3 = RC[1]   (1 column right+)

Cell B2 = R[-1]C  (1 row above-)
Cell B4 = R[1]C   (1 row below+)
```

A few more examples:

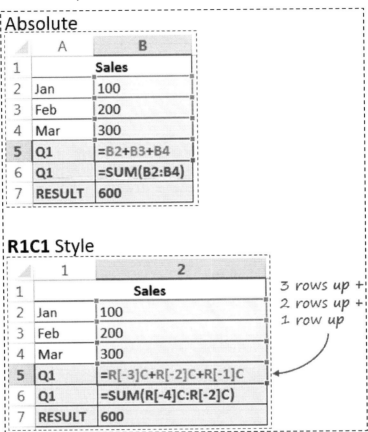

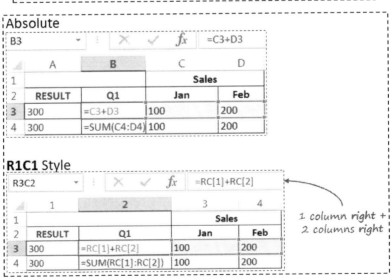

When recording a macro that uses a sum formula, it is represented as `FormulaR1C1`:

`ActiveCell.FormulaR1C1` =

You also have the option to *manually change VBA* code to use `Formula`:

`ActiveCell.Formula` =

Below are a few examples of how this works, each macro will insert a sum formula into the three cells. **Column 'D'** illustrates how the VBA code appears.

	A	B	C	D
1	Sales			
2	Jan	Feb	TOTAL	VBA EXAMPLE OF SUM FORMULA
3	100	200	=A3+B3	`Range("C3").Select` `ActiveCell.FormulaR1C1 = "=RC[-2]+RC[-1]"`
4	100	200	=SUM(A4:B4)	`Range("C4").Select` `ActiveCell.FormulaR1C1 = "=SUM(RC[-2]:RC[-1])"`
5	100	200	=SUM(A5:B5)	`Range("C5").Select` `ActiveCell.Formula = "=SUM(A5:B5)"`

Manually changed the code to use **Formula** (absolute)

	A	B	C
1	Sales		VBA EXAMPLE OF SUM FORMULA
2	Jan	100	
3	Feb	200	
4	TOTAL	=B2+B3	`Range("B4").Select` `ActiveCell.FormulaR1C1 = "=R[-2]C+R[-1]C"`
5	TOTAL	=SUM(B2:B3)	`Range("B5").Select` `ActiveCell.FormulaR1C1 = "=SUM(R[-3]C:R[-2]C)"`
6	TOTAL	=SUM(B2:B3)	`Range("B6").Select` `ActiveCell.Formula = "=SUM(B2:B3)"`

CHAPTER 7

How to use the 'Debug' tools

While recording macros reduces the occurrence of errors, you'll eventually need to address a change in process or troubleshoot an error with your macros. There are two types of macro errors:

1. Program errors
2. Logic errors

Program Errors

Program errors occur when the macro cannot finish. One or more errors exist in the VBA code and when executed, cause the program to fail or "break." With these types of errors, you'll always receive an error message, the macro will run until the error causes the program to stop at which point an error message will be displayed. An example of a common error message is:

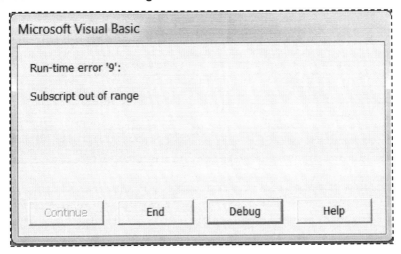

Program errors are easier to troubleshoot, because they show you exactly where the error is located. When you click the **'Debug'** button on the error prompt, it will open the VBA Editor and highlight with a yellow arrow where the program is failing.

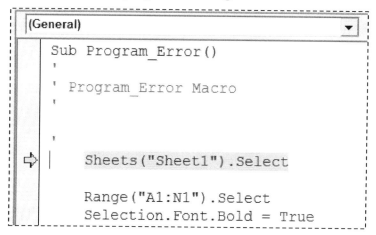

WEB ADDRESS & FILE NAME FOR EXERCISE:
http://bentonexcelbooks.my-free.website/macro-exercise-files
Chapter07_DebugTools.xlsm

Let's walk through an example:

1. Open the above file and click the **'Program Error'** button on the tab labeled **'Macros'**.

2. The macro *will error*, click on the **'Debug'** button on the error prompt

This error is being caused because the tab is named *'Program'* instead of *'Sheet1'*. To resolve, either change the tab name to *'Sheet1'* or the VBA code for sheets to *'Program'*. The best practice is to change the VBA code.

3. To make the VBA code modifications, change:
   - From: Sheets("Sheet1").Select
   - To: Sheets("Program").Select

4. From the Ribbon select '**Run** : **Reset**'

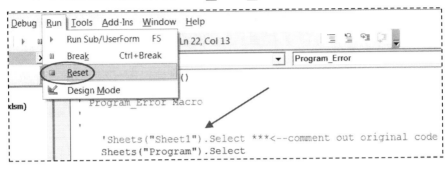

5. Change `("Sheet1") TO: Sheets("Program").Select`

6. **Save** the macro, if you receive the following message:

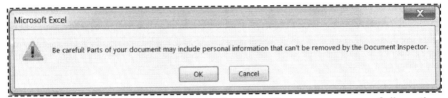

You may click the **'OK'** button to bypass the message or follow the instructions outlined in Appendix A to launch the **'Document Inspector'** feature within Excel® to inspect the document

7. Go back to the **'Macros'** tab and click the **'Program Error'** button *or* from the VBA editor Ribbon select '**Run** : **RunSub/UserForm F5**'

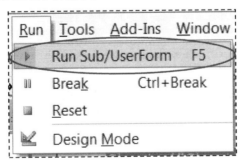

The macro should now run without error.

Logic Errors

Logic errors are more difficult to troubleshoot, because the macro will run without stopping or generating an error message. However, the end result is not correct. This usually occurs when something changes to an existing process. A few examples include:

- New fields (rows or columns) are added to an existing report
- The row or column order is altered on an existing report
- The format of cells has changed on an existing report
- The time when an existing report is available has changed

With logic errors you do not receive an error message, therefore it can take longer to understand the root cause and implement a fix.

Let's walk through example. When we run the formatting macro we **expect** the result to be as follows:

	A	B	C	D	E	F	G	H	I	J	K	L	M	N
1	STORE	JAN	FEB	MAR	APR	MAY	JUN	JUL	AUG	SEP	OCT	NOV	DEC	TOTAL
2	Store 1	$ 211	$ 1,287	$ 726	$ 444	$ 1,039	$ 237	$ 785	$ 1,471	$ 1,418	$ 1,468	$ 522	$ 1,059	$ 10,667
3	Store 2	$ 782	$ 141	$ 1,023	$ 183	$ 331	$ 294	$ 567	$ 178	$ 538	$ 133	$ 477	$ 681	$ 5,328
4	Store 3	$ 278	$ 510	$ 427	$ 677	$ 526	$ 430	$ 1,091	$ 1,167	$ 1,349	$ 853	$ 689	$ 234	$ 8,231
5	Store 4	$ 1,085	$ 1,467	$ 1,298	$ 1,005	$ 642	$ 1,169	$ 742	$ 1,317	$ 827	$ 412	$ 458	$ 1,020	$ 11,442
6	Store 5	$ 112	$ 1,203	$ 561	$ 281	$ 378	$ 1,483	$ 741	$ 1,467	$ 896	$ 1,393	$ 291	$ 1,458	$ 10,284
7	Store 6	$ 488	$ 953	$ 518	$ 1,152	$ 1,214	$ 1,038	$ 972	$ 796	$ 1,272	$ 854	$ 224	$ 1,089	$ 10,570
8	Store 7	$ 991	$ 1,366	$ 1,220	$ 1,322	$ 1,222	$ 1,025	$ 975	$ 491	$ 320	$ 1,415	$ 636	$ 1,369	$ 12,352
9	Store 8	$ 998	$ 1,480	$ 1,173	$ 606	$ 1,058	$ 200	$ 202	$ 1,031	$ 518	$ 604	$ 826	$ 658	$ 9,354
10	Store 9	$ 360	$ 227	$ 533	$ 714	$ 942	$ 1,081	$ 1,499	$ 898	$ 765	$ 516	$ 369	$ 952	$ 8,856
11	Store 10	$ 1,296	$ 748	$ 434	$ 858	$ 1,234	$ 1,491	$ 1,358	$ 1,322	$ 1,093	$ 765	$ 213	$ 920	$ 11,672
12	Store 11	$ 753	$ 1,311	$ 495	$ 422	$ 259	$ 1,172	$ 630	$ 1,319	$ 1,383	$ 504	$ 1,083	$ 908	$ 10,439
13	Store 12	$ 114	$ 533	$ 141	$ 642	$ 547	$ 1,207	$ 773	$ 1,125	$ 278	$ 694	$ 196	$ 131	$ 6,386
14	Store 13	$ 1,339	$ 1,177	$ 1,377	$ 1,086	$ 1,165	$ 487	$ 824	$ 1,333	$ 988	$ 569	$ 1,021	$ 1,076	$ 12,442
15	Store 14	$ 1,082	$ 922	$ 406	$ 190	$ 247	$ 1,084	$ 783	$ 1,043	$ 1,233	$ 981	$ 1,261	$ 309	$ 10,041
16	Store 15	$ 525	$ 572	$ 399	$ 659	$ 667	$ 849	$ 950	$ 442	$ 1,358	$ 437	$ 1,338	$ 224	$ 8,420
17	Store 16	$ 364	$ 1,131	$ 1,217	$ 335	$ 261	$ 1,104	$ 798	$ 1,304	$ 421	$ 1,298	$ 131	$ 532	$ 8,896
18	Store 17	$ 653	$ 1,286	$ 1,487	$ 764	$ 185	$ 621	$ 1,015	$ 406	$ 301	$ 1,229	$ 777	$ 1,300	$ 10,024
19	Store 18	$ 698	$ 1,065	$ 280	$ 697	$ 517	$ 646	$ 1,115	$ 568	$ 156	$ 520	$ 1,084	$ 578	$ 7,924
20	Store 19	$ 1,151	$ 1,258	$ 1,201	$ 826	$ 1,294	$ 648	$ 936	$ 193	$ 1,137	$ 354	$ 803	$ 480	$ 10,281
21	Store 20	$ 469	$ 1,080	$ 613	$ 931	$ 391	$ 407	$ 482	$ 1,359	$ 384	$ 1,500	$ 1,241	$ 603	$ 9,460
22	Store 21	$ 1,331	$ 1,007	$ 303	$ 447	$ 1,315	$ 690	$ 721	$ 917	$ 1,191	$ 1,129	$ 1,177	$ 1,232	$ 11,460
23	Store 22	$ 1,295	$ 280	$ 1,317	$ 794	$ 276	$ 716	$ 988	$ 898	$ 1,493	$ 353	$ 367	$ 1,182	$ 9,959
24	Store 23	$ 1,207	$ 547	$ 1,030	$ 1,326	$ 338	$ 211	$ 304	$ 498	$ 526	$ 126	$ 225	$ 872	$ 7,210
25	Store 24	$ 1,421	$ 134	$ 1,030	$ 968	$ 145	$ 434	$ 1,332	$ 1,164	$ 492	$ 621	$ 366	$ 194	$ 8,301
26	Store 25	$ 1,294	$ 674	$ 117	$ 1,396	$ 1,012	$ 933	$ 1,026	$ 1,374	$ 1,383	$ 969	$ 669	$ 1,343	$ 12,190

1. Open the above file and click the '**Logic Error**' button on the tab labeled '**Macros**'.

2. The macro *will run*, but notice the format is incorrect

	A	B	C	D	E	F	G	H	I	J	K	L	M	N
1	tore Sales													TOTAL
2	STORE	JAN	FEB	MAR	APR	MAY	JUN	JUL	AUG	SEP	OCT	NOV	DEC	$
3	Store 1	$ 211	$ 1,287	$ 726	$ 444	$ 1,039	$ 237	$ 785	$ 1,471	$ 1,418	$ 1,468	$ 522	$ 1,059	$ 10,667
4	Store 2	$ 782	$ 141	$ 1,023	$ 183	$ 331	$ 294	$ 567	$ 178	$ 538	$ 133	$ 477	$ 681	$ 5,328
5	Store 3	$ 278	$ 510	$ 427	$ 677	$ 526	$ 430	$ 1,091	$ 1,167	$ 1,349	$ 853	$ 689	$ 234	$ 8,231
6	Store 4	$ 1,085	$ 1,467	$ 1,298	$ 1,005	$ 642	$ 1,169	$ 742	$ 1,317	$ 827	$ 412	$ 458	$ 1,020	$ 11,442
7	Store 5	$ 112	$ 1,203	$ 561	$ 281	$ 378	$ 1,483	$ 741	$ 1,467	$ 896	$ 1,393	$ 291	$ 1,458	$ 10,264
8	Store 6	$ 488	$ 953	$ 518	$ 1,152	$ 1,214	$ 1,038	$ 972	$ 796	$ 1,272	$ 854	$ 224	$ 1,089	$ 10,570
9	Store 7	$ 991	$ 1,366	$ 1,220	$ 1,322	$ 1,222	$ 1,025	$ 975	$ 491	$ 320	$ 1,415	$ 636	$ 1,369	$ 12,352
10	Store 8	$ 998	$ 1,480	$ 1,173	$ 606	$ 1,058	$ 200	$ 202	$ 1,031	$ 518	$ 604	$ 826	$ 658	$ 9,354
11	Store 9	$ 360	$ 227	$ 533	$ 714	$ 942	$ 1,081	$ 1,499	$ 898	$ 765	$ 516	$ 369	$ 952	$ 8,856
12	Store 10	$ 1,296	$ 748	$ 434	$ 858	$ 1,234	$ 1,491	$ 1,358	$ 1,322	$ 1,033	$ 765	$ 213	$ 920	$ 11,672
13	Store 11	$ 753	$ 1,311	$ 495	$ 422	$ 259	$ 1,172	$ 830	$ 1,319	$ 1,383	$ 504	$ 1,083	$ 908	$ 10,439
14	Store 12	$ 114	$ 533	$ 141	$ 647	$ 547	$ 1,207	$ 773	$ 1,125	$ 278	$ 694	$ 196	$ 131	$ 6,386
15	Store 13	$ 1,339	$ 1,177	$ 1,377	$ 1,086	$ 1,165	$ 487	$ 824	$ 1,333	$ 988	$ 569	$ 1,021	$ 1,076	$ 12,442
16	Store 14	$ 1,082	$ 922	$ 406	$ 190	$ 247	$ 1,084	$ 783	$ 1,043	$ 1,233	$ 981	$ 1,261	$ 809	$ 10,041
17	Store 15	$ 525	$ 572	$ 399	$ 659	$ 667	$ 849	$ 950	$ 442	$ 1,358	$ 437	$ 1,338	$ 224	$ 8,420
18	Store 16	$ 364	$ 1,131	$ 1,217	$ 335	$ 261	$ 1,104	$ 798	$ 1,304	$ 421	$ 1,298	$ 131	$ 532	$ 5,896
19	Store 17	$ 653	$ 1,286	$ 1,487	$ 764	$ 185	$ 621	$ 1,015	$ 406	$ 301	$ 1,229	$ 777	$ 1,300	$ 10,024
20	Store 18	$ 698	$ 1,065	$ 280	$ 697	$ 517	$ 646	$ 1,115	$ 568	$ 156	$ 520	$ 1,084	$ 578	$ 7,924
21	Store 19	$ 1,151	$ 1,258	$ 1,201	$ 826	$ 1,294	$ 648	$ 936	$ 193	$ 1,137	$ 354	$ 803	$ 480	$ 10,281
22	Store 20	$ 469	$ 1,080	$ 613	$ 931	$ 391	$ 407	$ 482	$ 1,359	$ 384	$ 1,500	$ 1,241	$ 603	$ 9,460
23	Store 21	$ 1,331	$ 1,007	$ 303	$ 447	$ 1,315	$ 690	$ 721	$ 917	$ 1,191	$ 1,129	$ 1,177	$ 232	$ 11,460
24	Store 22	$ 1,295	$ 280	$ 1,317	$ 794	$ 278	$ 716	$ 988	$ 898	$ 1,493	$ 353	$ 367	$ 1,392	$ 9,959
25	Store 23	$ 1,207	$ 547	$ 1,030	$ 1,326	$ 338	$ 211	$ 304	$ 498	$ 526	$ 126	$ 225	$ 877	$ 7,210
26	Store 24	$ 1,421	$ 134	$ 1,030	$ 968	$ 145	$ 434	$ 1,332	$ 1,164	$ 492	$ 621	$ 366	$ 194	$ 8,301
27	Store 25	1294	674	117	1396	1012	933	1026	1374	1383	969	669	1343	

3. Close the file **WITHOUT SAVING**

Reopen the file and examine the '**Program**' tab and then the '**Logic**' tab. You'll see the '**Logic**' tab has an extra row (row1) inserted called '**Store Sales**'.

Program tab:

	A	B	C	D	E
1	STORE	JAN	FEB	MAR	APR
2	Store 1	211	1287	726	444
3	Store 2	782	141	1023	183

Logic tab:

	A	B	C	D	Extra row with title has been added
1	**Store Sales**				
2	STORE	JAN	FEB	MAR	APR
3	Store 1	211	1287	726	444
4	Store 2	782	141	1023	183

It won't always be so obvious what has changed, this is where the VBA debugging tools are especially helpful.

4. Open the VBA Editor for the '**Logic_Error**' macro (**Module2**)

5. Place your cursor right before the word '**Sub**'

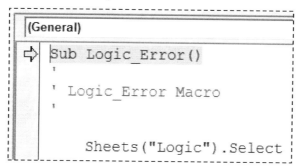

6. From the Ribbon select '**Debug : Step Into F8**'

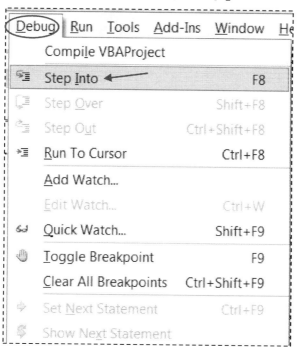

You'll notice how the first line of code is highlighted with a yellow arrow. While in debug mode, the macro will proceed through the code, step-by-step. It will pause after each step and you can watch how each line performs a specific action.

7. Press **'F8'** on your keyboard or click the **'Step Into'** icon

We can watch each step of the macro being completed:

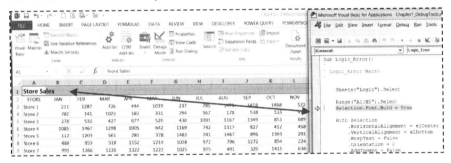

8. Continue to press **'F8'** on your keyboard or **'Step Into'** icon

As you progress, you'll begin to see where the code the needs to be modified. Often when recording macros, the main issue will be related to cell ranges no longer being correct.

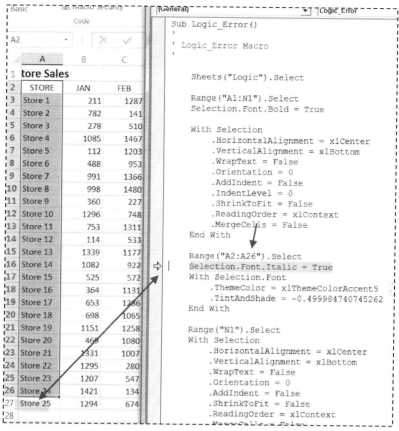

Once you understand the root cause of why your macro is not producing the correct results, you can then decide on how you want to resolve the issue(s). With most macros, you'll have a number of different options for resolution. Your approach will depend on the situation, your audience, experience, and time. In this example, I see three possible options:

1. Start over, record a new macro that accommodates the newly inserted line of text

2. Manually change the required code to address the newly inserted line of text

3. Add code that deletes the first row, allowing the macro to run as originally coded

In this case, there is no option with a real advantage over another. When evaluating your options factor in time, testing, and business value.

☑ A few more VBA Debugging Tools:

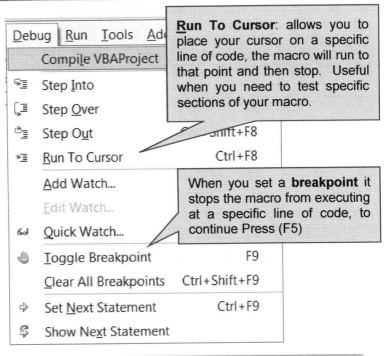

Controlled Error Messages

If you're developing macros for another department or someone else will be using a program you created, you may want to control the error message they see if a program error occurs. These message boxes allow you to communicate with your customer and guide them to an appropriate support resource. Also, you won't run the risk of them clicking the **'Debug'** button and potentially changing your code.

While message boxes can't be recorded the code can be copied and incorporated into the macros you record:

1. Open the file **'Chapter07_DebugTools.xlsm'**

2. Select the tab labeled '**MessageBox**'

3. Click the **'Display Message'** button

4. The macro **will error** and the below message will display where the customer can go for assistance

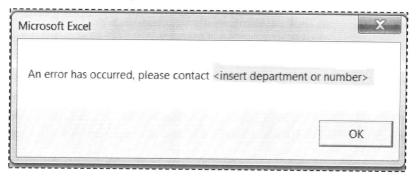

Code Review

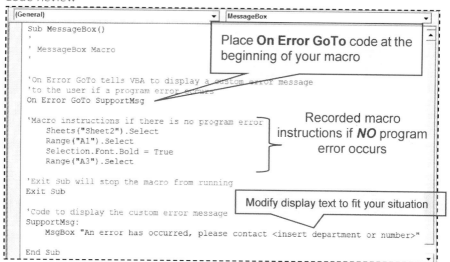

☑ **Additional Information:**

On Error GoTo will execute the instructions of the macro until a program error occurs. Meaning, the macro may be 1/2 or 1/3 complete before an error, this could cause some processes to be incomplete and have unintended results.

CHAPTER 8

Report macro #1 – recording a macro to format a monthly report

MACRO OBJECTIVES

- Develop a macro that converts a *detailed* database file into a monthly *summary* report

SCENARIO:

As a member of the Administrative Support staff, you produce a regional summary report each month. You're given a detailed database Excel® file. The column headers are the database table field names and there are several hundred individual records. You decide to create a macro that will:

1. Create a summary tab with only the required columns

2. Add subtotal functionality to summarize each region's sales detail

---

MACRO LIMITATIONS:

The macro assumes your cell ranges, number of records (rows & columns) *stay constant*. Chapter 11 'Introduction To Loop Structures', addresses variable record counts.

WEB ADDRESS & FILE NAME FOR EXERCISE:

http://bentonexcelbooks.my-free.website/macro-exercise-files

Chapter08_ReportFormatting.xlsx

EXAMPLE:
Take the following report:

A portion of a detailed database report (provided every month for the previous month's data).

Please Note:

- *The column headers appear to be the database field names*
- *There is a MONTH_ID instead of a month name or date*

	A	B	C	D	E	F	G	H	I	J
1	SALES_REGION_ID	SALES_REGION_NAME	SALES_PERSON_ID	SLS_PRSN_FULL_NM	CATEGORY_ID	CATEGORY_NA	PART_ID	PART_NAME	MONTH_ID	QTY_SOLD
2	1	Central	100	Smith, John	1	STRUCTURAL	2339	Pressure Bulkheads	2	2
3	1	Central	100	Smith, John	1	STRUCTURAL	1344	Keel Beam	2	8
4	1	Central	100	Smith, John	1	STRUCTURAL	1084	Fuselage Panels	2	1
5	1	Central	100	Smith, John	2	FUEL	4828	Boost Pumps	2	2
6	1	Central	100	Smith, John	2	FUEL	1703	Transfer Valves	2	5
7	1	Central	100	Smith, John	2	FUEL	3089	Fuel S.O.V.	2	3
8	1	Central	100	Smith, John	2	FUEL	3836	Digital Fuel Flow Sys	2	8
9	1	Central	100	Smith, John	2	FUEL	1277	Fuel Quantity Indica	2	8
10	1	Central	100	Smith, John	2	FUEL	4779	Fuel Flow Indicating	2	4
11	1	Central	100	Smith, John	2	FUEL	4679	Fuel Pressure Indica	2	9

Transform into a formatted summary report:

	A	B
1	**Monthly Summary**	
2	**February 2016**	
3	**REGION**	**QTY SOLD**
112	**Central Total**	569
221	**East Total**	596
330	**West Total**	588
331	**Grand Total**	1,753
332		

STEPS TO RECORD MACRO

1. Open the file: **Chapter08_ReportFormatting.xlsx**

2. Click the **'Record Macro'** field, (please see chapter 4, page 21 if you're unfamiliar with how to do this).
   - **Name** the macro: **'Monthly_Summary'**
   - Verify the **'Store macro in:'** has **'This Workbook'** selected in the drop-down box

3. **Create a Worksheet Copy** of '**Sheet1**' *(a good best practice to always have the original data to refer back to)*

4. Rename '**Sheet1 (2)**' to '**Monthly Summary**'

5. Delete **column 'A'**

6. Delete **columns(B:G)**

7. Insert a row (above row 1)

8. In the newly inserted row 1, cell '**A1**' apply the below formula. This will convert the month number into a text month and year:
   - `=TEXT(DATE(2016,B3,1),"mmmm_yyyy")`

9. **Copy** and **Paste As A Value** the formula in cell '**A1**'
   This will allow us to delete the month column and not affect our month formula

10. Delete **column 'B'**

11. Change cell text in '**A2**' from '**SALES_REGION_NAME**' to '**REGION**'

12. Change cell text in '**B2**' from '**QTY_SOLD**' to '**QTY SOLD**'

13. Select cells '**A2:B326**' and insert the **Subtotal function**, from the Ribbon select DATA : Subtotal
    A. At each change in: REGION
    B. Use function: Sum
    C. Add subtotal to: QTY SOLD
    D. Click the 'OK' button

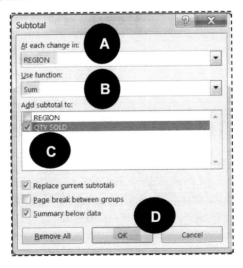

14. Display the summary data by clicking the **#2**

1 2 3		A	B
	1	February 2016	
	2	REGION	QTY SOLD
+	111	**Central Total**	569
+	220	**East Total**	596
+	329	**West Total**	588
−	330	**Grand Total**	1753

15. Select cells **'B111:B330'** and change to **number format**, zero decimals

16. Select cells **'A2:B2'** and change format to **bold**

17. Insert a row (above row 1)

18. Insert the text **'Monthly Summary'** into cell **'A1'**

19. **Bold** cells **'A1:A2'**

20. **Merge & Center** cell **'A1'** across columns **'A'** & **'B'**

21. **Merge & Center** cell **'B1'** across columns **'A'** & **'B'**

22. **Increase font size** of cells **'A1:A2'** to Calibri 16

23. Click the **'Stop Recording'** field

24. **Save** the workbook as a **macro file** (please see chapter 4, page 27 if you're unfamiliar with how to do this).

If you receive the following message:

You may click the **'OK'** button to bypass the message or follow the instructions outlined in Appendix A to launch the **'Document Inspector'** feature within Excel® to inspect the document

---

To test the macro:

1. If closed, open the *macro* file:
   Chapter08_ReportFormatting.xlsm

2. Delete the tab named **'Monthly Summary'**

3. Run the macro 'Monthly_Summary'

CODE REVIEW

Steps 1 - 12

```
(General)                           ▼   Monthly_Summary                        ▼

    Sub Monthly_Summary()
    '
    ' Monthly_Summary Macro
    '

    'Step #3 Copy 'Sheet1'
        Sheets("Sheet1").Select
        Sheets("Sheet1").Copy After:=Sheets(1)

    'Step #4 Rename 'Sheet1 (2)' to 'Monthly Summary'
        Sheets("Sheet1 (2)").Select
        Sheets("Sheet1 (2)").Name = "Monthly Summary"

    'Step #5 Delete column 'A'
        Columns("A:A").Select
        Selection.Delete Shift:=xlToLeft

    'Step #6 Delete columns(B:G)
        Columns("B:G").Select
        Selection.Delete Shift:=xlToLeft

    'Step #7 Insert a row (above row 1)
        Rows("1:1").Select
        Selection.Insert Shift:=xlDown, CopyOrigin:=xlFormatFromLeftOrAbove
```

```
(General)                           ▼   Monthly_Summary                        ▼

    'Step #8 In the newly inserted row 1 apply the formula to convert the
    '         the month number to a text month and year
        Range("A1").Select
        ActiveCell.FormulaR1C1 = "=TEXT(DATE(2016,R[2]C[1],1),""mmmm_yyyy"")"

    'Step #9 Copy and Paste As A Value the formula in cell 'A1'
    '         This will allow us to delete the month column and not
    '         affect our month formula
        Range("A1").Select
        Selection.Copy
        Selection.PasteSpecial Paste:=xlPasteValues, Operation:=xlNone, SkipBlanks _
            :=False, Transpose:=False

    'Step #10 Delete column 'B'
        Columns("B:B").Select
        Application.CutCopyMode = False
        Selection.Delete Shift:=xlToLeft

    'Step #11 Change cell text in 'A2' from 'SALES_REGION_NAME' to 'REGION'
        Range("A2").Select
        ActiveCell.FormulaR1C1 = "REGION"

    'Step #12 Change cell text in 'B2' from 'QTY_SOLD' to 'QTY SOLD'
        Range("B2").Select
        ActiveCell.FormulaR1C1 = "QTY SOLD"
        Range("A2:B2").Select
```

Excel® Macros & VBA
For Business Users - A Beginners Guide

Steps 13 - 21

```
'Step #13 Insert Subtotal function, select cells 'A2:B326'
'           From the ribbon select DATA : Subtotal
    Range(Selection, Selection.End(xlDown)).Select
    Range("A2:B326").Select
    Selection.Subtotal GroupBy:=1, Function:=xlSum, TotalList:=Array(2), _
        Replace:=True, PageBreaks:=False, SummaryBelowData:=True

'Step #14 Display subtotal summary data - Level 2
    Range("A1").Select
    ActiveSheet.Outline.ShowLevels RowLevels:=2

'Step # 15 Select cells 'B111:B330' and change to number format, zero decimals
    Range("B111:B330").Select
    Selection.Style = "Comma"
    Selection.NumberFormat = "_(* #,##0.0_);_(* (#,##0.0);_(* ""-""??_);_(@_)"
    Selection.NumberFormat = "_(* #,##0_);_(* (#,##0);_(* ""-""??_);_(@_)"

'Step #16 Select cells 'A2:B2' and change format to bold
    Range("A2:B2").Select
    Selection.Font.Bold = True

'Step # 17 Insert a row (above row 1)
    Rows("1:1").Select
    Selection.Insert Shift:=xlDown, CopyOrigin:=xlFormatFromLeftOrAbove

'Step #18 Insert the text 'Monthly Summary' into cell 'A1'
    Range("A1").Select
    ActiveCell.FormulaR1C1 = "Monthly Summary"

'Step #19 Bold cells 'A1:A2'
    Range("A1:A2").Select
    Selection.Font.Bold = True
```

(General) ▼   Monthly_Summary ▼

```
'Step #20 Merge & Center cell 'A1' across columns 'A' & 'B'
    Range("A1:B1").Select
    With Selection
        .HorizontalAlignment = xlCenter
        .VerticalAlignment = xlBottom
        .WrapText = False
        .Orientation = 0
        .AddIndent = False
        .IndentLevel = 0
        .ShrinkToFit = False
        .ReadingOrder = xlContext
        .MergeCells = False
    End With
    Selection.Merge

'Step #21. Merge & Center cell 'B1' across columns 'A' & 'B'
    Range("A2:B2").Select
    With Selection
        .HorizontalAlignment = xlCenter
        .VerticalAlignment = xlBottom
        .WrapText = False
        .Orientation = 0
        .AddIndent = False
        .IndentLevel = 0
        .ShrinkToFit = False
        .ReadingOrder = xlContext
        .MergeCells = False
    End With
    Selection.Merge
```

Step 22

```
'Step #22 Increase font size of cells 'A1:A2' to Calibri = 16
    Range("A1:B2").Select
    With Selection.Font
        .Name = "Calibri"
        .Size = 16
        .Strikethrough = False
        .Superscript = False
        .Subscript = False
        .OutlineFont = False
        .Shadow = False
        .Underline = xlUnderlineStyleNone
        .ThemeColor = xlThemeColorLight1
        .TintAndShade = 0
        .ThemeFont = xlThemeFontMinor
    End With

    Range("A332").Select
End Sub
```

CHAPTER 9

Data Analysis Macro – analyzing test results

MACRO OBJECTIVES

- Inserting formulas
- Applying conditional formatting
- Inserting new worksheets

SCENARIO:

You're a Quality Assurance Analyst working on a data migration project. You're responsible for comparing the results between an old and new airline parts system. You have been informed you may have to complete between 75 – 100 tests. The following are the requirements for each iteration:

1. Compare the results of the two systems, they need to match exactly. Using a formula, identify the records that do not match.

2. Highlight with shading the records that DO NOT MATCH between the two systems.
   a. Apply an AutoFilter to allow for easy identification of the records that do not match.

3. Insert a tab with the following information:
   a. Provides a summary of the test results
   b. Identifies the date and time the test was completed

MACRO LIMITATIONS:
This macro assumes your cell ranges, number of records (rows) *stay constant*. Chapter 11 'Introduction To Loop Structures', addresses variable record counts.

WEB ADDRESS & FILE NAME FOR EXERCISE:
http://bentonexcelbooks.my-free.website/macro-exercise-files
Chapter09_DataAnalysis.xlsx

EXAMPLE:
From:

	A	B	C	D
1	PART #	NEW SYSTEM	OLD SYSTEM	
2	Part #1	878	878	
3	Part #2	944	944	
4	Part #3	796	796	
5	Part #4	222	222	
6	Part #5	614	614	
7	Part #6	149	145	
8	Part #7	621	621	
9	Part #8	937	937	
10	Part #9	107	107	
11	Part #10	665	665	
12	Part #11	108	108	
3999	Part #3998	909	909	
4000	Part #3999	689	689	
4001	Part #4000	841	841	

To: (parts 1 & 2)

	A	B	C	D
1	PART #	NEW SYSTEM	OLD SYSTEM	COMPARSION
2	Part #1	878	878	Match
3	Part #2	944	944	Match
4	Part #3	796	796	Match
5	Part #4	222	222	Match
6	Part #5	614	614	Match
7	Part #6	149	145	No Match
8	Part #7	621	621	Match
9	Part #8	937	937	Match
10	Part #9	107	107	Match

... Testing Summary | **Testing Results** | (+)

EXAMPLE Continued.....

TO: (part 3)

	A	B	C
1	**Testing Summary**		
2	Number of Records	4000	99.9%
3	Number of Records That Match	3978	99.5%
4	Number of Records That DO NOT MATCH	17	0.4%
5			
6	Testing Completed	1/15/2016 9:54	
7			
8			
9			
10			

◄ ► ... | **Testing Summary** | Testing Results | ⊕ : ◄

STEPS TO RECORD MACRO

(PART 1):

1. Open the file: **Chapter09_DataAnalysis.xlsx**

2. Click the **'Record Macro'** field, (please see chapter 4, page 21 if you're unfamiliar with how to do this).
   - **Name** the macro: **'DataAnalysis'**
   - Verify the **'Store macro in:'** has **'This Workbook'** selected in the drop-down box

3. Rename tab **'Sheet1'** to **'Original'**

4. **Create a Worksheet Copy** of newly named **'Original'** worksheet and name it **'Testing Results'**

5. On the newly created **'Testing Results'** worksheet, label cell **'D1'** **'COMPARISON'**

6. Insert the *'IF'* formula `=IF(B2=C2,"Match","No Match")` to cells **'D2:,D4001'**

STEPS (PART 2):

7. Apply conditional formatting to **column 'D'**

    - From the Ribbon select **HOME : Conditional Formatting**

    - Select **Highlight Cells Rules → Equal To...**

    - When dialogue box appears enter:

        1) In the 'Format cells that are **EQUAL TO**: box enter **'No Match'**

        2) In the **'with'** box, click the drop-down box and select '**Light Red Fill with Dark Red Text'**

    - Click the 'OK' button

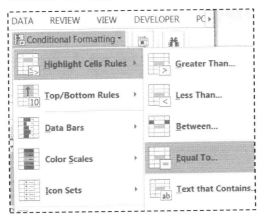

8. Apply **AutoFilter** to columns **'A:D'**, this will allow your customers to filter by color.

STEPS (PART 3):

9. Insert a new worksheet and **NAME** it **'Testing Summary'** *(we'll be updating this section of code in step #28)*

10. Cell '**A1**' add text '**Testing Summary**'

11. Cell **'A2'** add text '**Number of Records'**

12. Cell **'A3'** add text '**Number of Records That Match**'

13. Cell **'A4'** add text '**Number of Records That DO NOT Match**'

14. Change the **Column 'A'** width to **35**, by **right clicking Column 'A'** and selecting the '**Column Width…**'option

15. Cell **'B2'** insert formula:
    - `=COUNTA('Testing Results'!A2:A4001)`

16. Cell **'B3'** insert formula:
    - `=COUNTIF('Testing Results'!D2:D4001,"Match")`

17. Cell **'B4'** insert formula:
    - `=COUNTIF('Testing Results'!D2:D4001,"No Match")`

18. Cell **'C2'** insert formula:
    - `=SUM(C3:C4)`

19. Cell **'C3'** insert formula:
    - `=B3/B2`

20. Cell **'C4'** insert formula:
    - `=B4/B2`

21. Change the formatting for cells '**C2:C4**' to **percent** with one decimal point

22. Bold and merge center across columns '**A1:C1**' '**Testing Summary**'

23. Cell **'A6'** add text '**Testing Completed:**'

24. Cell **'B6'** add formula:
    - `=NOW()`

25. Cell **'B6' Copy** and **Paste As a Value**

26. Select cell **'A7'** and press the **'ESC'** on your keyboard

27. Click the **'Stop Recording'** button

28. Open the **VBA Editor** *(from the Ribbon select **DEVELOPER** : Visual Basic)* and locate the following three lines of code *(step #9 from above)*:

```
Sheets.Add After:=ActiveSheet
Sheets("Sheet2").Select
Sheets("Sheet2").Name = "Testing Summary"
```

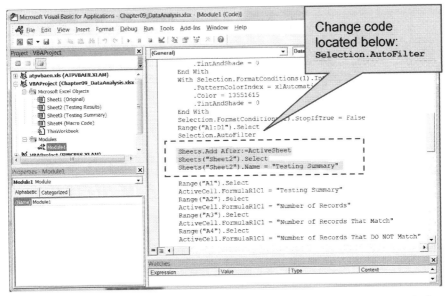

29. Comment out the above three lines of code and add the following two lines:

```
Sheets.Add
ActiveSheet.Name = "Testing Summary"
```

```
Selection.AutoFilter

'What was recorded (comment out):
'    Sheets.Add After:=ActiveSheet
'    Sheets("Sheet2").Select
'    Sheets("Sheet2").Name = "Testing Summary"
*NEW CODE*
Sheets.Add
ActiveSheet.Name = "Testing Summary" '****SHOULD BE THE ACTIVE CODE*****


Range("A1").Select
ActiveCell.FormulaR1C1 = "Testing Summary"
```

30. **Save** the workbook as a **macro file** (please see chapter 4, page 27 if you're unfamiliar with how to do this).

If you receive the following message:

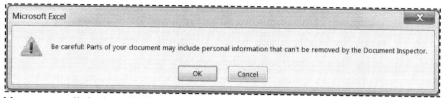

You may click the **'OK'** button to bypass the message or follow the instructions outlined in <u>Appendix A</u> to launch the **'Document Inspector'** feature within Excel® to inspect the document

---

To test the macro:
1. If closed, open the *macro* file:
   Chapter09_DataAnalysis.xlsm
2. Delete the two worksheets **'Testing Summary'** & **'Testing Results'**
3. Rename **'Original'** tab to **'Sheet1'**
4. Run the macro **'DataAnalysis'**

CODE REVIEW

Part 1

```
Sub DataAnalysis()

' DataAnalysis Macro

'***********************************************************************
'   PART 1
'***********************************************************************

'Step#3 = Rename 'Sheet1' to 'Original'
    Sheets("Sheet1").Select
    Sheets("Sheet1").Name = "Original"

'Step#4 = Copy newly named 'Original' sheet, name it 'Testing Results'
    Sheets("Original").Select
    Sheets("Original").Copy After:=Sheets(1)
    Sheets("Original (2)").Select
    Sheets("Original (2)").Name = "Testing Results"

'Step#5 = On the newly created 'Testing Results' sheet,
'         label cell 'D1' 'COMPARISON'
    Range("D1").Select
    ActiveCell.FormulaR1C1 = "COMPARSION"
    Range("D1").Select

'Step#6 = Apply "if" formula IF(B2=C2,"Match","No Match") to cells 'D2:,D4001'
    Columns("D:D").EntireColumn.AutoFit
    Range("D2").Select
    ActiveCell.FormulaR1C1 = "=IF(RC[-2]=RC[-1],""Match"",""No Match"")"
    Range("D2").Select
    Selection.Copy
    Range("D3:D4001").Select
    ActiveSheet.Paste
    Application.CutCopyMode = False
```

Part 2

```
'**************************************************************
'   PART 2
'**************************************************************

'Step#7 = Apply conditional formatting to column 'D'
    Columns("D:D").Select
    Selection.FormatConditions.Add Type:=xlCellValue, Operator:=xlEqual, _
        Formula1:="=""No Match"""
    Selection.FormatConditions(Selection.FormatConditions.Count).SetFirstPriority
    With Selection.FormatConditions(1).Font
        .Color = -16383844
        .TintAndShade = 0
    End With
    With Selection.FormatConditions(1).Interior
        .PatternColorIndex = xlAutomatic
        .Color = 13551615
        .TintAndShade = 0
    End With
    Selection.FormatConditions(1).StopIfTrue = False

'Step#8 = Apply AutoFilter to columns 'A:D'
    Range("A1:D1").Select
    Selection.AutoFilter
    Cells.Select
    Cells.EntireColumn.AutoFit
    Range("G13").Select
```

Part 3

```
'**************************************************************
'   PART 3
'**************************************************************
'Step#9 = Insert new tab ***THIS SECTION OF CODE IS MANUALLY CHANGED*****
    'What was recorded (comment out):
    '    Sheets.Add After:=ActiveSheet        Modify this
    '    Sheets("Sheet3").Select              section of code
    '    Sheets("Sheet3").Name = "Testing Summary"
    '*NEW CODE (manually add)*
    Sheets.Add
    ActiveSheet.Name = "Testing Summary" '****SHOULD BE THE ACTIVE CODE*****

'Steps #10 - 13 = Inserting text descriptions
    Range("A1").Select
    ActiveCell.FormulaR1C1 = "Testing Summary"

    Range("A2").Select
    ActiveCell.FormulaR1C1 = "Number of Records"

    Range("A3").Select
    ActiveCell.FormulaR1C1 = "Number of Records That Match"

    Range("A4").Select
        ActiveCell.FormulaR1C1 = "Number of Records That DO NOT MATCH"

    Range("A5").Select

'Step#14 = change the column width
    Columns("A:A").ColumnWidth = 35
```

Part 3 (continued):

```
'Steps #15 - 17 = Inserting COUNTA and COUNTIF formulas
    Range("B2").Select
    ActiveCell.FormulaR1C1 = "=COUNTA('Testing Results'!RC[-1]:R[4001]C[-1])"

    Range("B3").Select
    ActiveCell.FormulaR1C1 = _
        "=COUNTIF('Testing Results'!R[4]C[2]:R[4001]C[2],""Match"")"

    Range("B4").Select
        ActiveCell.FormulaR1C1 = _
        "=COUNTIF('Testing Results'!R[-2]C[2]:R[4001]C[2],""No Match"")"

'Steps #18 - 20 = Inserting SUM and % formulas
    Range("C4").Select
    ActiveCell.FormulaR1C1 = "=RC[-1]/R[-2]C[-1]"

    Range("C3").Select
    ActiveCell.FormulaR1C1 = "=RC[-1]/R[-1]C[-1]"

    Range("C2").Select
    ActiveCell.FormulaR1C1 = "=SUM(R[1]C:R[2]C)"

'Step 21 = Change the formatting for cells 'C2:C4'
'          to percent w/ one decimal point
    Range("C2:C4").Select
    Selection.Style = "Percent"
    Selection.NumberFormat = "0.0%"
```

```
'Step#22 = Bold and merge center across columns 'A1:C1'
    Range("A1:C1").Select
    Selection.Font.Bold = True
    With Selection
        .HorizontalAlignment = xlCenter
        .VerticalAlignment = xlBottom
        .WrapText = False
        .Orientation = 0
        .AddIndent = False
        .IndentLevel = 0
        .ShrinkToFit = False
        .ReadingOrder = xlContext
        .MergeCells = False
    End With
    Selection.Merge

'Step 23 = Cell 'A6' add text 'Testing Completed'
    Range("A6").Select
    ActiveCell.FormulaR1C1 = "Testing Completed"

'Step 24 = Cell 'B2' add formula =NOW
    Range("B6").Select
    ActiveCell.FormulaR1C1 = "=NOW()"

'Step 25 = Cell 'B2' copy and paste as a value
    Range("B6").Select
    Selection.Copy
    Selection.PasteSpecial Paste:=xlPasteValues, Operation:=xlNone, SkipBlanks _
        :=False, Transpose:=False
    Application.CutCopyMode = False

    Range("A7").Select

End Sub
```

CHAPTER 10

Using macros and Pivot Tables to parse text or .CSV files

Like with many tasks in Excel®, file parsing can be accomplished in multiple ways. The following examples demonstrate two methods for reading and parsing text and .CSV (comma separated value) files and then transforming the parsed data into a formatted Excel® report.

MACRO OBJECTIVES (file type = text)

- Parse and format a text file using a macro
- Add a macro button to update (refresh) the data

SCENARIO:

As a member of the Administrative Support staff, you produce a formatted employee sales report each month.

Employee sales are captured in a legacy system. This older system produces a monthly *text file* and saves it to a company server location. To save time formatting the same report each month you create a macro to:

1. Parse the text file and format the data into a Excel® report
2. Add a button to the report to easily launch the macro

WEB ADDRESS & FILE NAMES FOR EXERCISE:
http://bentonexcelbooks.my-free.website/macro-exercise-files
1. EmployeeSales.txt
2. Chapter10_TextFileParse.xlsx

EXAMPLE:
From:

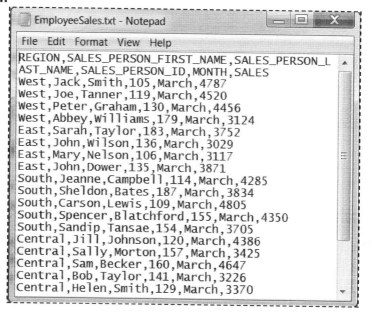

To:

	A	B	C	D	E	F
1	REGION	FIRST NAME	LAST NAME	ID	MONTH	SALES
2	West	Jack	Smith	105	March	£ 4,787
3	West	Joe	Tanner	119	March	£ 4,520
4	West	Peter	Graham	130	March	£ 4,456
5	West	Abbey	Williams	179	March	£ 3,124
6	East	Sarah	Taylor	183	March	£ 3,752
7	East	John	Wilson	136	March	£ 3,029
8	East	Mary	Nelson	106	March	£ 3,117
9	East	John	Dower	135	March	£ 3,871
10	South	Jeanne	Campbell	114	March	£ 4,285
11	South	Sheldon	Bates	187	March	£ 3,834
12	South	Carson	Lewis	109	March	£ 4,805
13	South	Spencer	Blatchford	155	March	£ 4,350
14	South	Sandip	Tansae	154	March	£ 3,705
15	Central	Jill	Johnson	120	March	£ 4,386
16	Central	Sally	Morton	157	March	£ 3,425
17	Central	Sam	Becker	160	March	£ 4,647
18	Central	Bob	Taylor	141	March	£ 3,226
19	Central	Helen	Smith	129	March	£ 3,370

STEPS TO RECORD MACRO (text file – part #1)

1. Create a new blank Excel® spreadsheet **(CTRL + N)**

2. Rename **'Sheet1'** to **'Employee Sales Report'**

3. Select cell **'A1'** *(make the active cell)*

4. Click the **'Record Macro'** field, (please see chapter 4, page 21 if you're unfamiliar with how to do this).
   - **Name** the macro: **'EmpSalesTextFileParse'**
   - Verify the **'Store macro in:'** has **'This Workbook'** selected in the drop-down box

5. **Click on** the worksheet tab **'Employee Sales Report'**

6. From the Ribbon select **DATA : Get External Data : From Text**

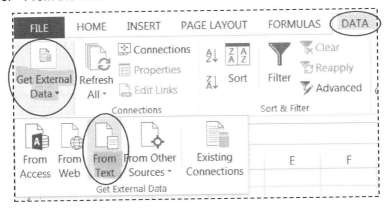

7. When prompted select the file path you created where the file **'EmployeeSales.txt'** is located. This book is using:

   C:\MacroTrainingBook\Chapter10\EmployeeSales.txt

8. Select the **'EmployeeSales.txt'** file and click the **'Import'** button

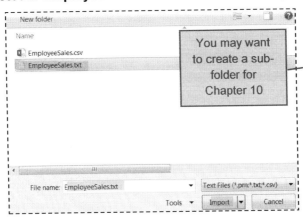

You may want to create a sub-folder for Chapter 10

The following **Text Import Wizard** will be displayed:

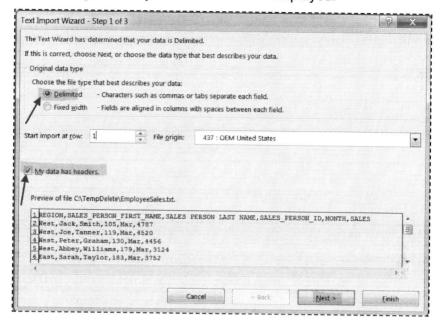

9. Select the **'Delimited'** radio button and **'My data has headers'** check box

10. Click the **'Next>'** button

Step 2 of the **Text Import Wizard** will be displayed:

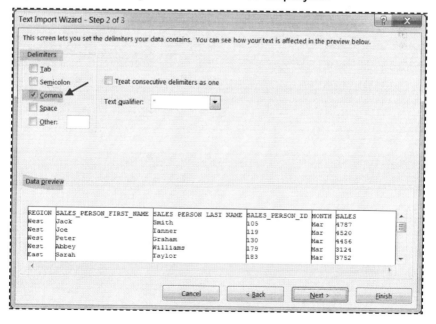

11. For the Delimiters, select the '**Comma**' check box

12. Click the '**Finish**' button

The following prompt will appear:

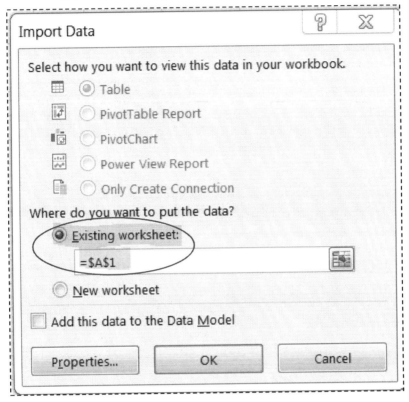

13. Select the '**Existing worksheet:**' radio button

14. Verify **=$A$1** is entered in the **Existing worksheet:**' field

15. Click the '**OK**' button

The text data should now be loaded into Excel®:

	A	B	C	D	E	F
1	REGION	SALES_PERSON_FIRST_NAME	SALES_PERSON_LAST_NAME	SALES_PERSON_ID	MONTH	SALES
2	West	Jack	Smith	105	March	4787
3	West	Joe	Tanner	119	March	4520
4	West	Peter	Graham	130	March	4456
5	West	Abbey	Williams	179	March	3124
6	East	Sarah	Taylor	183	March	3752
7	East	John	Wilson	136	March	3029
8	East	Mary	Nelson	106	March	3117

16. Select cells **'A1:F1'** and change format to **BOLD**

17. Cell **'B1'** *FROM* **'SALES_PERSON_FIRST_NAME'** *TO* **'FIRST NAME'**

18. Cell **'C1'** *FROM* **'SALES_PERSON_LAST_NAME'** *TO* **'LAST NAME'**

19. Cell **'D1'** *FROM* **'SALES_PERSON_ID'** *TO* **'ID'**

20. Select cells **'A1:F1'** and **CENTER** text

21. Select column **'F'** and change to your preferred **currency type**, with **zero decimal places**. *The British Pound £ was selected for this demonstration*

22. AutoFit columns **'A:D'**
    - Select **Columns 'A:D'**
    - From the **Home Tab** select **Cells → Format**
    - Under '**Cell Size**', click '**AutoFit Column Width**'

23. Select cell **'A1'**

24. Stop Recording

25. Open the **VBA Editor** *(from the Ribbon select DEVELOPER : Visual Basic)*

26. **Locate** and **comment out** the following line of code:
    `.CommandType = 0`

*CommandType is used for QueryTable objects and since we're importing a **text file**, this line of code doesn't apply to our macro.*

27. Save the workbook as a **macro file** (please see chapter 4, page 27 if you're unfamiliar with how to do this).

    You may want to name something like:
    Chapter10_TextFileParse.xlsm

To test the macro:

1. If closed, open the *macro* file you created in step #27 above. This book created file: **Chapter10_TextFileParse.xlsm**

2. Place your cursor in **cell 'H1'**

3. **Select All (CTRL+A)** from the worksheet **'Employee Sales Report'**

4. **DELETE** the data by pressing the **'Delete' button** on your keyboard

You'll receive the following message:

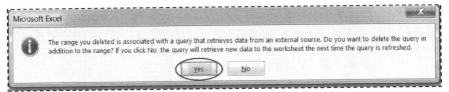

5. Click the **'Yes'** button

6. Run the macro **'EmpSalesTextFileParse'**

The results should be similar to the following:

	A	B	C	D	E	F
1	REGION	FIRST NAME	LAST NAME	ID	MONTH	SALES
2	West	Jack	Smith	105	March	£ 4,787
3	West	Joe	Tanner	119	March	£ 4,520
4	West	Peter	Graham	130	March	£ 4,456
5	West	Abbey	Williams	179	March	£ 3,124
6	East	Sarah	Taylor	183	March	£ 3,752
7	East	John	Wilson	136	March	£ 3,029
8	East	Mary	Nelson	106	March	£ 3,117
9	East	John	Dower	135	March	£ 3,871
10	South	Jeanne	Campbell	114	March	£ 4,285
11	South	Sheldon	Bates	187	March	£ 3,834
12	South	Carson	Lewis	109	March	£ 4,805
13	South	Spencer	Blatchford	155	March	£ 4,350
14	South	Sandip	Tansae	154	March	£ 3,705
15	Central	Jill	Johnson	120	March	£ 4,386
16	Central	Sally	Morton	157	March	£ 3,425
17	Central	Sam	Becker	160	March	£ 4,647
18	Central	Bob	Taylor	141	March	£ 3,226
19	Central	Helen	Smith	129	March	£ 3,370

CODE REVIEW

Steps 5 – 15

```
Sub EmpSalesTextFileParse()
'
' EmpSalesTextFileParse Macro

'STEP #5 Click on the worksheet tab 'Employee Sales Report'
Sheets("Employee Sales Report").Select

'STEPS #6 - 15 Imports and parses the text file
With ActiveSheet.QueryTables.Add(Connection:= _
    "TEXT;C:\MacroTrainingBook\Chapter10\EmployeeSales.txt", Destination:=Range( _
    "$A$1"))
    '.CommandType = 0 ***See instructions from the book step#26***
    .Name = "EmployeeSales"
    .FieldNames = True
    .RowNumbers = False
    .FillAdjacentFormulas = False
    .PreserveFormatting = True
    .RefreshOnFileOpen = False
    .RefreshStyle = xlInsertDeleteCells
    .SavePassword = False
    .SaveData = True
    .AdjustColumnWidth = True
    .RefreshPeriod = 0
    .TextFilePromptOnRefresh = False
    .TextFilePlatform = 437
    .TextFileStartRow = 1
    .TextFileParseType = xlDelimited
    .TextFileTextQualifier = xlTextQualifierDoubleQuote
    .TextFileConsecutiveDelimiter = False
    .TextFileTabDelimiter = False
    .TextFileSemicolonDelimiter = False
    .TextFileCommaDelimiter = True
    .TextFileSpaceDelimiter = False
    .TextFileColumnDataTypes = Array(1, 1, 1, 1, 1, 1)
    .TextFileTrailingMinusNumbers = True
    .Refresh BackgroundQuery:=False
    End With
```

> **Comment out this line of code**

CommandType *is used for QueryTable objects and since we're importing a* **text file**, *this line of code doesn't apply to our macro.*

Code review continued on next page......

Steps 16 - 20

```
'STEP #16 Select cells 'A1:F1' and change format to BOLD
    Range("A1:F1").Select
    Selection.Font.Bold = True

'STEPS #17 - 19 change cell text values
    Range("B1").Select
    ActiveCell.FormulaR1C1 = "FIRST NAME"

    Range("C1").Select
    ActiveCell.FormulaR1C1 = "LAST NAME"

    Range("D1").Select
    ActiveCell.FormulaR1C1 = "ID"

'STEP #20 Select cells 'A1:F1' and CENTER text
    Range("A1:F1").Select
    With Selection
        .HorizontalAlignment = xlCenter
        .VerticalAlignment = xlBottom
        .WrapText = False
        .Orientation = 0
        .AddIndent = False
        .IndentLevel = 0
        .ShrinkToFit = False
        .ReadingOrder = xlContext
        .MergeCells = False
    End With
```

Steps 21 -23

```
'STEP #21 Select column 'F' and change to your preferred currency type,
'          with zero decimal places
    Columns("F:F").Select
    Selection.NumberFormat = _
        "_-[$£-809]* #,##0.00_-;-[$£-809]* #,##0.00_-;_-[$£-809]* ""-""??_-;_-@_-"
    Selection.NumberFormat = _
        "_-[$£-809]* #,##0.0_-;-[$£-809]* #,##0.0_-;_-[$£-809]* ""-""??_-;_-@_-"
    Selection.NumberFormat = _
        "_-[$£-809]* #,##0_-;-[$£-809]* #,##0_-;_-[$£-809]* ""-""??_-;_-@_-"

'STEP #22 AutoFit all columns
    Cells.Select
    Cells.EntireColumn.AutoFit

'STEP #23 Select cell 'A1'
    Range("A1").Select

End Sub
```

STEPS TO RECORD MACRO (text file – part #2)

Before adding the **macro button**, we need to record another macro to delete the old report data. We will then prepend the new delete macro to the existing **'EmpSalesTextFileParse'** or whatever you named it. To begin verify the report data from the **'EmpSalesTextFile'** macro has executed and there is report data in the worksheet **'Employee Sales Report'**.

1. Click the **'Record Macro'** field, (please see chapter 4, page 21 if you're unfamiliar with how to do this).
   - **Name** the macro: **'DeleteReportData'**
   - Verify the **'Store macro in:'** has **'This Workbook'** selected in the drop-down box
2. **Click on** the worksheet tab **'Employee Sales Report'**
3. Place your cursor in **cell 'H1'**
4. **Select All (CTRL+A)** from the worksheet from the worksheet **'Employee Sales Report'**
5. **DELETE** the data by pressing the **'Delete' button** on your keyboard

You'll receive the following message:

6. Click the **'Yes'** button
7. Place your cursor in cell **'A1'**
8. Stop Recording
9. Save the macro and file

To test the macro:

1. Run the **'EmpSalesTextFile'** macro
2. Run the **'DeleteReportData'** macro
3. Verify both macros are working as expected

Now that we have the **DeleteReportData'** macro, we'll merge the two macros together.

To begin verify the report data from the **'EmpSalesTextFileParse'** macro has executed and there is report data in the worksheet **'Employee Sales Report'**.

1. Open the **VBA Editor** *(from the Ribbon select **DEVELOPER** : **Visual Basic**)*
2. Locate the **'DeleteReportData'** macro
3. **Locate** and **comment out** the following line of code: `Selection.QueryTable.Delete`
4. **Copy** the following lines code of code:

```
'DeleteReportData Macro
    Sheets("Employee Sales Report").Select
    Cells.Select
    Range("H1").Activate
    'Selection.QueryTable.Delete  *Comment out*
    Selection.ClearContents
    Range("A1").Select
```

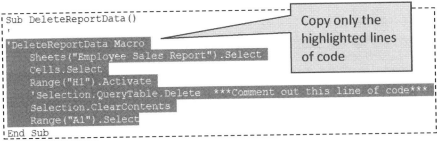

5. Locate the code for the **"EmpSalesTextFileParse'** macro
6. **Paste** the copied lines **above** the code line:

`Sheets("Employee Sales Report").Select`

```
Sub EmpSalesTextFileParse()
'
' EmpSalesTextFileParse Macro

'DeleteReportData Macro
    Sheets("Employee Sales Report").Select
    Cells.Select
    Range("H1").Activate
    'Selection.QueryTable.Delete  ***Comment out this line of code***
    Selection.ClearContents
    Range("A1").Select

Sheets("Employee Sales Report").Select

With ActiveSheet.QueryTables.Add(Connection:= _
    "TEXT;C:\MacroTrainingBook\Chapter10\EmployeeSales.txt", Destinatio
    "$A$1"))
```

7. Save the file

8. Test the updated **'EmpSalesTextFile'** macro

The result should delete the old report and populate with the new data.

Adding a macro button (controls)
Return to the worksheet **'Employee Sales Report'**

1. From Ribbon select **DEVELOPER : Insert**

2. From the **'Insert'** drop-down box, under **'Form Controls'** select the **rectangular button**

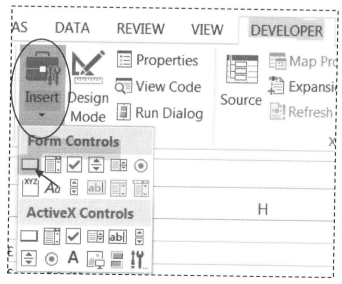

3. Draw the button near cell **'H2'**, you'll be prompted to **Assign a Macro**

A prompt *similar* to the below will be displayed:

4. Select **'EmpSalesTextFileParse'**

5. Click the **'OK'** button

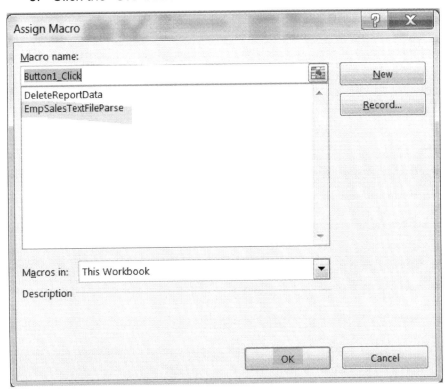

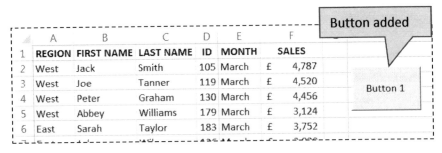

6. You may edit the text by **right clicking** on the button and selecting **'Edit Te_xt'**

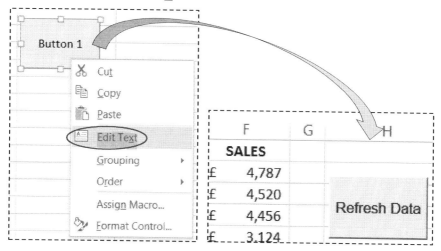

7. Test the button, by adding rows to the text file

8. Click the button and the new data should be added

PIVOT TABLE OBJECTIVES (file type = .CSV)

- Parse and format a .CSV file using Pivot Tables

SCENARIO:

The management staff has requested a change to a monthly employee sales report. Management would now like to see a regional summary and employee sales *grouped* and *subtotaled by region.*

Employee sales are captured in a legacy system. This older system produces a monthly *.CSV file* and saves it to a company server location. To save time formatting the same report each month you create Pivot Tables to:

1. Parse the .CSV file and format the data into a Excel® report. The below example does not involve macro recording, instead demonstrates how Pivot Tables can be used to create automated reporting without the level of complexity and maintenance required by

C.J. Benton

macros.

As this example will show, you can accomplish the same degree of automation and robust report formatting with Pivot Tables as with macros, but Pivot Tables require less time to develop, test, and maintain.

WEB ADDRESS & FILE NAMES FOR EXERCISE:
http://bentonexcelbooks.my-free.website/macro-exercise-files
1. EmployeeSales.csv

EXAMPLE:
From:

100

To:

	A	B	C	D	E	F
1	Employee & Region Sales Report					
2						
3	**EMPLOYEE & REGION**	**MONTH** ⁻			**REGION**	**MONTH** ⁻
4	**SALES** ⁻	**March**			**SALES** ⁻	**March**
5	⊟ **Central**	**19,054**			Central	19,054
6	Becker	4,647			East	13,769
7	Johnson	4,386			South	20,979
8	Morton	3,425			West	16,887
9	Smith	3,370			**TOTAL**	**70,689**
10	Taylor	3,226				
11	⊟ **East**	**13,769**				
12	Dower	3,871				
13	Nelson	3,117				
14	Taylor	3,752				
15	Wilson	3,029				
16	⊟ **South**	**20,979**				
17	Bates	3,834				
18	Blatchford	4,350				
19	Campbell	4,285				
20	Lewis	4,805				
21	Tansae	3,705				
22	⊟ **West**	**16,887**				
23	Graham	4,456				
24	Smith	4,787				
25	Tanner	4,520				
26	Williams	3,124				
27	**TOTAL**	**70,689**				

STEPS TO CREATE PIVOT TABLE (.CSV file)

1. Create a new blank Excel® spreadsheet **(CTRL + N)**

2. Rename **'Sheet1'** to **'Monthly Sales Report'**

3. Select cell **'A1'** and enter the text **'Employee & Region Sales Report'**

4. Select cell **'A3'**

5. From the Ribbon select **INSERT** : **PivotTable**

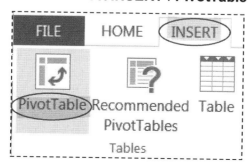

The following dialogue box will appear:

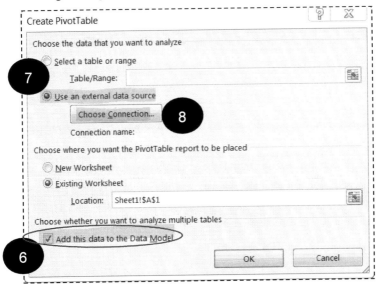

6. Click the **'Add this data to the Data Model'** checkbox

7. Select the **'Use an external data source'** radio button

8. Click the **'Choose Connection…'** button

A prompt *similar* to the following should appear:

9. Click the '**Browse for More…**' button

10. When prompted select the file path you created where file '**EmployeeSales.csv**' is located. This book is using: **C:\MacroTrainingBook\Chapter10\EmployeeSales.csv**

11. Click the '**Open**' button

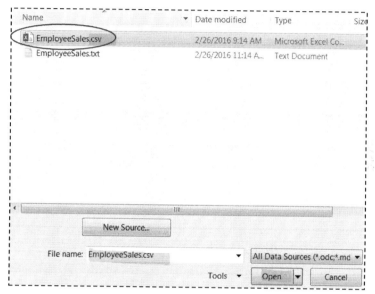

The following **Text Import Wizard** will be displayed:

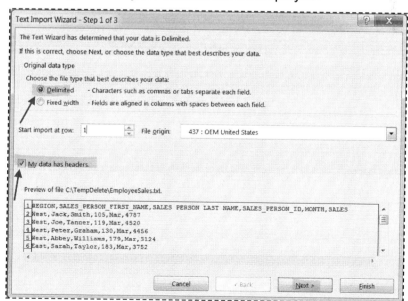

12. Select the **'Delimited'** radio button and **'<u>My data has</u> <u>headers</u>'** check box

13. Click the **'<u>Next></u>'** button

Step 2 of the **Text Import Wizard** will be displayed:

14. For the Delimiters, select the **'<u>Comma</u>'** check box

15. Click the **'<u>Finish</u>'** button

The following prompt will appear:

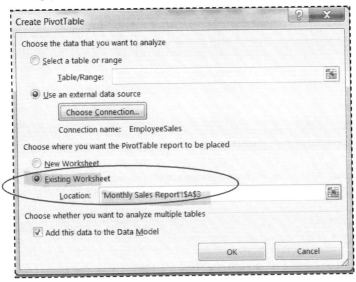

16. Click the **'OK'** button

A prompt similar to the following should appear *(it may take moment to load)*:

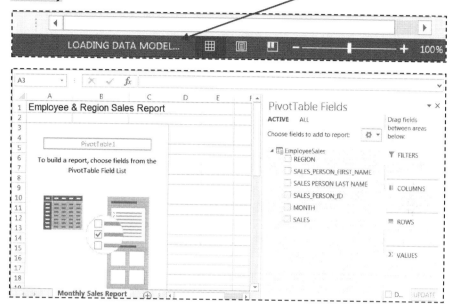

17. Select the following PivotTable fields:

- **Columns** = MONTH
- **Rows:** = REGION & SALES PERSON LAST NAME
- **Values:** = SALES

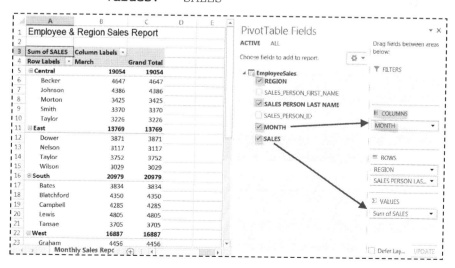

18. Place your cursor in cell **'E3'**

19. Repeat steps 5 – 8 from above

A prompt similar to the following should appear:

20. Select **'EmployeeSales'** and click the **'Open'** button

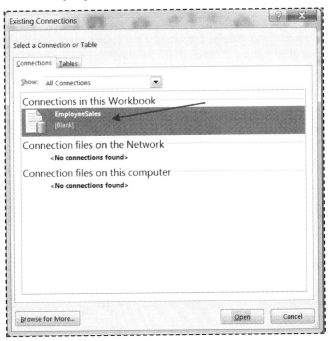

21. Click the **'OK'** button

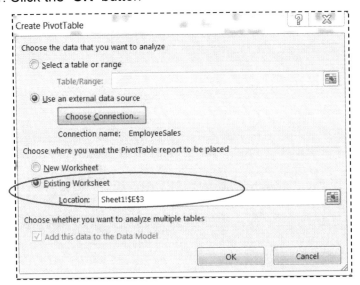

22. Create and format a new Pivot Table:
- Columns = MONTH
- Rows: = REGION
- Values: = SALES

23. Right click over *both* '**Grand Total**' fields and select '**Remove Grand Total**'

24. Re-label and format column headings, change currency to your preference

You may also define refresh properties

1. Click on any Pivot Table field to activate the **'PIVOTTABLE TOOLS'** toolbar

2. From the **'PIVOTTABLE TOOLS'** toolbar **select**
   - **ANALYZE : Refresh : Connection Properties...**

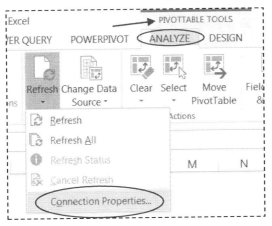

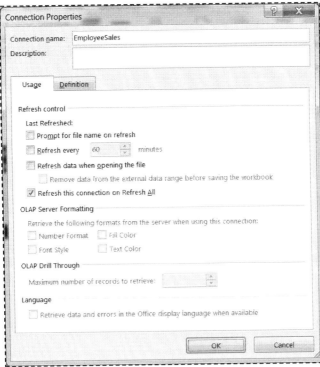

Example using Pivot Table styles and charts to enhance report:

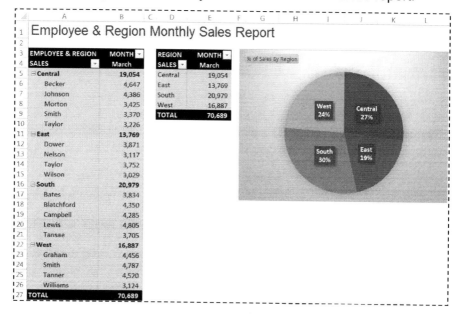

***

If you would like to learn more about Pivot Tables, please check out my book: The Step-By-Step Guide To Pivot Tables & Introduction To Dashboards

The book contains several basic, intermediate, and advanced Pivot Table examples with screenshots demonstrating how to:

- Organize and summarize data
- Format results
- Inserting both bar and pie Pivot Charts
- Displaying averages & percentages
- Grouping data into predefined ranges
- Ranking results
- Inserting calculated fields

In addition to the above, you will also learn **how to create and update a basic Dashboard** using Pivot Table data.

CHAPTER 11

Introduction To Loop Structures

Looping is the process of repeating a set of code instructions based on a specific condition. Looping allows you to work with data of varying lengths and inconsistent formats. By incorporating a loop structure into your macros, you will be able to automate more tasks.

You may apply one or multiple loops in a single sub-procedure. Some examples of when loops are beneficial:

- ✓ Inserting formulas or text to an indeterminate number of records
- ✓ Applying transformational tasks to records, such as parsing cells or appending / prepending the content of cells
- ✓ Separating, copying, and writing records of a worksheet to separate tabs or files
- ✓ Looping through files in a directory and identifying those meeting a specific criteria. Such as those that contain words like "budget," "forecast," or "SOP"

However, adding loops does require programming, more testing, and increased maintenance. It can also be a little intimidating to learn at first. Therefore, I've attempted to make it easier to understand by focusing on only *two* types of loops: **'For Each...Next'** and **'Do...Loop'**.

If you would like to learn more about VBA loop structures than what is offered in this chapter, please visit Microsoft's® website for more information on the subject, the URL is:

https://msdn.microsoft.com/en-us/library/ezk76t25(v=vs.140).aspx

The four VBA Microsoft® loop structures are:

LOOP STRUCTURE	
Do...Loop	Repeats a set of statements an indefinite number of times, *until* a condition is met or *while* condition exists.
For Each...Next	Executes one or more statements once for each element defined
While...End While	Similar to the 'Do...Loop', only repeats a set of statements as long as a condition remains true
For...Next	Repeats a set of statements for a limited number iterations

CAUTION!
Before we begin coding loops it is important to know, if a loop is not coded correctly, a macro may continuously run (loop), sometimes effecting the processing performance of your computer. **To stop a loop while in progress, press the 'ESC' (Escape) button on your keyboard *twice*.**

After pressing the 'ESC' (Escape) button on your keyboard twice, you'll receive the following prompt, **click the 'End' button**. This will stop the macro from continuing and allow you to fix your code.

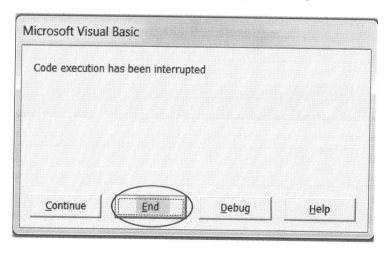

For Each...Next Loop

For Each...Next loops are one of the most frequently used types of loops, because they allow you to repeat specific instructions for each element defined, without having to know how many of those elements there are.

For example, earlier in this book (chapter 5) we created a macro to unhide all hidden worksheets of the active workbook. We don't know how many worksheets will be hidden at any given time, but the code we want executed, when this macro is launched, is for all hidden tabs (1 or more) to be unhidden.

We used the following 'For Each...Next' loop:

```
Dim WrkSheet As Worksheet

For Each WrkSheet In Sheets: WrkSheet.Visible = True: Next

End Sub
```

Let's take a closer look at the required syntax for a 'For Each...Next' loop:

```
For Each Element [ As datatype ] In [ Group ]

    [Statements]

Next
```

Element	Variable (datatype)
Group	Object or collection for statements to be applied
Statements	Action to be repeated on each object or collection
Next	Ends each loop

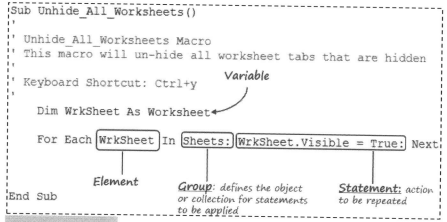

```
Sub Unhide_All_Worksheets()
'
' Unhide_All_Worksheets Macro
' This macro will un-hide all worksheet tabs that are hidden
'
' Keyboard Shortcut: Ctrl+y
'
    Dim WrkSheet As Worksheet
                                        ← Variable

    For Each WrkSheet In Sheets: WrkSheet.Visible = True: Next

End Sub
```

Element

Group: *defines the object or collection for statements to be applied*

Statement: *action to be repeated*

More Examples!

For another example of a 'For Each...Next' loop please see chapter 16. In chapter 16, the loop saves each worksheet as a separate workbook. Chapter 17 provides two examples of a 'For...Next' loop, demonstrating how to sort worksheets either alphabetically or numerically.

Do...Loop

A 'Do...Loop' is similar to a 'For Each...Next loop' in that it will allow you to repeat specific instructions for an indeterminate number of iterations. However, instead of repeating the set of code for each element defined, it will apply the statements *until* a condition **becomes** true **or** *while* a condition **is** true.

Conceptual diagram of Do...Loop types

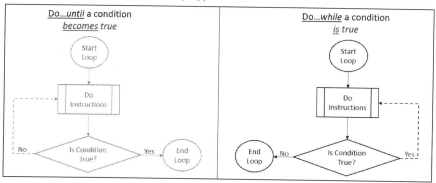

The required syntax for a 'Do...Loop':

```
Do [ While or Until ] condition

    [statements]

Loop
--------- OR ----------
Do

    [statements]

Loop [While or Until] condition
```

Do	Starts the loop
While	Repeat statements *while* a condition *is* true
Until	Repeat statements *until* a condition *becomes* true
Condition	Is the condition true or false?
Statements	Action to be repeated
Loop	Ends the loop

In each Do...Loop:

- ✓ You can only use either **While** or **Until,** but not both

- ✓ Each loop can test only one condition

- ✓ If you test the condition at the start of the loop (in the Do statement), the loop might not run even one time. If you test at the end of the loop (in the Loop statement), the loop always runs at least one time.

I've found it easier to learn the Do *Until* vs. the Do *While* loop, because the coding and readability is more intuitive.

For our first example, let's revisit the Data Analysis exercise discussed in chapter 9. If you recall, we applied an *'IF'* formula to a specific range of cells ('D2:'D4001') to compare if the values in columns 'B' & 'C' matched. However, we had a limitation in the macro. The macro would only work for a *specific number of records* ('D2:'D4001'). We'll enhance the macro to accommodate each iteration by inserting a 'Do...Loop' that will account for a variable number of records.

*Data Analysis example **(an 'IF' formula applied to column 'D' for all rows with a value in column 'A')':***

	A	B	C	D
1	PART # ▾	NEW SYSTEM ▾	OLD SYSTEM ▾	COMPARSION ▾
2	Part #1	878	878 Match	
3	Part #2	944	944 Match	
4	Part #3	796	796 Match	
5	Part #4	222	222 Match	
6	Part #5	614	614 Match	
7	Part #6	149	145 No Match	
8	Part #7	621	621 Match	
9	Part #8	937	937 Match	
10	Part #9	107	107 Match	

◀ ▶ ⋯ | Testing Summary | **Testing Results** | ⊕ | ◀

WEB ADDRESS & FILE NAME FOR EXERCISE:
http://bentonexcelbooks.my-free.website/macro-exercise-files
Chapter11_DoLoop.xlsx

STEPS TO CREATE MACRO

This **Do *Until*** loop macro cannot be recorded, the code will need to manually entered:

1. Open the file **Chapter11_DoLoop.xlsx**
2. Select the '**Developer**' tab
3. Click the **'Visual Basic'** field

The VBA Editor will open:

1. Make sure **'Chapter11_DoLoop.xlsx'** is selected (highlighted)

2. From the VBA Editor Ribbon select **'Insert : Module'**

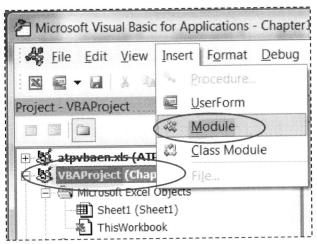

A new module should now be added:

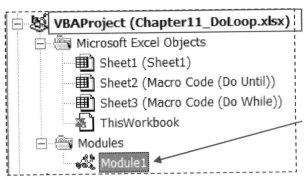

4. **Enter** or **copy and paste** the following lines of code from the **'Macro Code (Do Until)'** tab of the spreadsheet into the newly added module:

```
Sub Do_Until_Loop()

'The below is an example of a 'Do Until' loop
'The loop will apply a formula in column 'D' for all rows
'with a value in column 'A'
    Dim RowNum As Integer

    RowNum = 2

    Sheets("Sheet1").Select

    Do Until Cells(RowNum, 1).Value = ""
        Cells(RowNum, 4).Value = "=IF(RC[-2]=RC[-1],""Match"",""No Match"")"
        RowNum = RowNum + 1
    Loop

End Sub
```

5. Test the macro 'Do_Until_Loop'

Column 'D' should now have the *'IF'* formula applied to all rows that have a value in **column 'A'**.

CODE REVIEW

The benefits of the Do...Loop allow you to apply the *'IF'* formula to each row in column 'D' ***until*** a row in column 'A' ***is*** empty.

```
Sub Do_Until_Loop()

'The below is an example of a 'Do Until' loop
'The loop will apply a formula in column 'D' for all rows
'with a value in column 'A'
    Dim RowNum As Integer

    RowNum = 2

    Sheets("Sheet1").Select

    Do Until Cells(RowNum, 1).Value = ""
        Cells(RowNum, 4).Value = "=IF(RC[-2]=RC[-1],""Match"",""No Match"")"
        RowNum = RowNum + 1
    Loop

    End Sub
```

Variable — setting the variable to start on row 2

Condition: execute statement(s) until a row in column 'A' is empty

Increment each row by 1

Repeat this statement until the condition becomes true (a row in column 'A' is empty)

You will learn more about the **'Cells'** object in Chapters 12 – 15. The **'Cells'** object allows us to identify the row and column index of where we want a statement to be applied. For example, if we wanted to **bold** cell '**B3**' we could write the following:

```
Sub Cells_Syntax_Example()
        Row
        |
    Cells(3, 2).Font.Bold = True
              |
          Column

    'Same as recording
    Range("B3").Select
    Selection.Font.Bold = True

End Sub
```

The following example of a **Do *While*** loop, accomplishes the same functionality as the Do Until, but is written differently. It states the instructions will run *while* a row in column 'A' *is not* empty.

```
Sub Do_While_Loop()

'The below is an example of a 'Do While' loop
'The loop will apply a formula in column 'D' for all rows
'with a value in column 'A'

    Dim RowNum As Integer

    RowNum = 2

    Sheets("Sheet1").Select

    Do While Cells(RowNum, 1).Value <> ""
        Cells(RowNum, 4).Value = "=IF(RC[-2]=RC[-1],""Match"",""No Match"")"
        RowNum = RowNum + 1
    Loop

'End_Sub
```

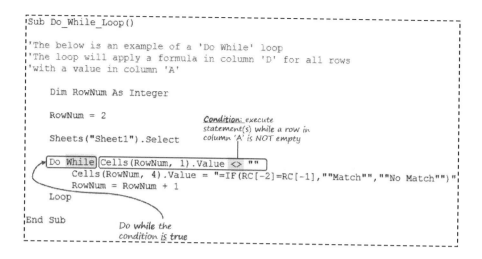

```
Sub Do_While_Loop()

'The below is an example of a 'Do While' loop
'The loop will apply a formula in column 'D' for all rows
'with a value in column 'A'

    Dim RowNum As Integer

    RowNum = 2

    Sheets("Sheet1").Select

    Do While Cells(RowNum, 1).Value <> ""
        Cells(RowNum, 4).Value = "=IF(RC[-2]=RC[-1],""Match"",""No Match"")"
        RowNum = RowNum + 1
    Loop

End Sub
```

Condition: execute statement(s) while a row in column 'A' is NOT empty

Do while the condition is true

I realize the difference between the **'Do...Until'** and **'Do...While'** is slight. I have not found any best practices or rules as to which is better to use when. The subtle differences are a matter of personal preference, however I've found the **'Do...Until'** to be a little easier to comprehend.

CHAPTER 12

How to use IF...THEN...ELSE and Select...Case Statements in macros

If...Then...Else and **Case Statements** are what Microsoft® refers to as **'Decision Structures'**. These structures allow you to test one or more conditions and perform a specific action depending on the result of the condition(s) being tested.

A basic **If...Then...Else** structure in VBA, essentially performs the same functionality as an 'IF' formula in a Excel® worksheet. Applying one statement if a condition is *true* and another statement if *false*. The If...Then...Else construct can be nested just like an 'IF' formula and apply multiple statements depending on the result of the conditions being tested.

A **Select...Case** structure in VBA, is similar to a nested 'IF' formula. It too will apply one or more statements contingent upon the value in the test, however the coding of a Select...Case is much easier to write and maintain.

The functionality of **If...Then...Else** and **Select...Case Statements** extend the power of looping, because they allow you to apply different actions as you loop through and evaluate each record independently.

For the examples in this chapter, we'll again be revisiting the Data Analysis exercise introduced in chapter 9. However, instead of applying an *'IF'* formula to a specific range of cells (i.e. 'D2:'D4001'), I will demonstrate three Decision Structures:

1. If...Then...Else
2. If...Then...ElseIF...Else
3. Select...Case

Illustration of the output of each decision structure:

PART #	NEW SYSTEM	OLD SYSTEM	VARIANCE	IF...THEN...ELSE	If...Then...Elself..Else	SELECT...CASE
Part #1	878	878		Match	Match	System Match 100%
Part #2	946	952	-6	No Match	Margin of Error greater than +/- 5	Variance greater than +/- 5
Part #3	796	800	-4	No Match	Acceptable w/in Margin	Pass OLD Sys =< 5
Part #4	222	220	2	No Match	Acceptable w/in Margin	Pass NEW Sys =< 5
Part #5	614	614		Match	Match	System Match 100%
Part #6	149	145	4	No Match	Acceptable w/in Margin	Pass NEW Sys =< 5
Part #7	621	621		Match	Match	System Match 100%

The required syntax for a basic **IF...THEN...ELSE** structure:

```
If Condition   Then
      [ statements ]
Else
      [ Else Statements ]
End If
```

Condition	A true or false statement
Statements	Action to be applied if true
Else Statements	Action to be applied if false
End If	Ends the If...Then...Else test

STEPS TO CREATE MACRO (Basic IF...THEN...ELSE)
This basic **If...Then...Else** macro cannot be recorded, the code will need to manually entered:

1. Open the file **Chapter12_If_Then_Case_Statements.xlsx**
2. Select the '**Developer**' tab
3. Click the **'Visual Basic'** field
4. Make sure '**Chapter12_If_Then_Case_Statements.xlsx**' is selected (highlighted)
5. From the VBA Editor Ribbon select '**Insert : Module**'

A new module should now be added

6. **Enter** or **copy and paste** the following lines of code from the **'IF_THEN_ELSE'** tab of the spreadsheet into the newly added module:

	Sheet1	IF_THEN_ELSE	IF_THEN_ELSEIF_ELSE	SELECT_CASE

```
Sub If_Then_Else()

'This is a Basic If...Then...Else macro
'It compares each row with values in columns 'B' and 'C'
'If the values match, the text "Match" will be inserted into column 'E'
'If the values DO NOT match, the text "No Match" will be inserted into column 'E'

    Dim RowNum As Integer
    Dim NewSys As Integer
    Dim OldSys As Integer
    Dim Result As String

    RowNum = 2

    Sheets("Sheet1").Select

    Do Until Cells(RowNum, 1).Value = ""

        NewSys = Cells(RowNum, 2).Value
        OldSys = Cells(RowNum, 3).Value

            If NewSys = OldSys Then
                Result = "Match"
            Else
                Result = "No Match"

            End If

        Cells(RowNum, 5).Value = Result

    RowNum = RowNum + 1

    Loop

End Sub
```

7. Test the macro `If_Then_Else`

Column 'E' should now have the value of **'Match'** or **'No Match'**.

CODE REVIEW (Basic IF...THEN...ELSE)

You're probably thinking why would anyone do all this extra typing instead of just inserting a 'IF' formula into column 'D', like we did in chapter 11's 'Do...Loop' examples. As we progress, you'll begin to see how performing this analysis in the macro enables us to complete more advanced data evaluations.

```
Sub If_Then_Else()

'This is a Basic If...Then...Else macro
'It compares each row with values in columns 'B'
'If the values match, the text "Match" will be ins
'If the values DO NOT match, the text "No Match"
        Variables
    Dim RowNum As Integer
    Dim NewSys As Integer
    Dim OldSys As Integer
    Dim Result As String

    RowNum = 2

    Sheets("Sheet1").Select

    Do Until Cells(RowNum, 1).Value = ""

        NewSys = Cells(RowNum, 2).Value
        OldSys = Cells(RowNum, 3).Value
        If NewSys = OldSys Then
            Result = "Match"
        Else
            Result = "No Match"

        End If

        Cells(RowNum, 5).Value = Result

    RowNum = RowNum + 1

    Loop

End Sub
```

Condition: the true or false expression
Action to be applied if **True**
Action to be applied if **False**

For the next example, let's expand our analysis to understand the degree in which the values between the new and old system do not match. Perhaps due to the way each system processes the data *slight variances, such as disparities of five or less are acceptable.*

The required syntax for an **If…Then…ElseIf…Else** structure:

```
If Condition   Then
    [ statements ]
ElseIf Condition   Then
    [ ElseIF Statements ]
Else
    [ Else Statements ]
End If
```

Condition	A true or false statement
Statements	Action to be applied if true
ElseIf Condition	A true or false statement
ElseIf Statements	Action to be applied if true
Else Statements	Action to be applied if false
End If	Ends the If...Then...Else test

FILE FOR EXERCISE:
Chapter12_If_Then_Case_Statements.xlsx

STEPS TO CREATE MACRO (If…Then…ElseIf…Else)
This **If…Then…ElseIf…Else** macro cannot be recorded, the code will need to manually entered:

1. Open the file **Chapter12_If_Then_Case_Statements.xlsx**
2. Select the '**Developer**' tab
3. Click the '**Visual Basic**' field
4. Make sure '**Chapter12_If_Then_Case_Statements.xlsx**' is selected (highlighted)
5. From the VBA Editor Ribbon select '**Insert : Module**'

A new module should now be added

6. **Enter** or **copy and paste** the following lines of code from the **'IF_THEN_ELSEIF_ELSE'** tab of the spreadsheet into the newly added module:

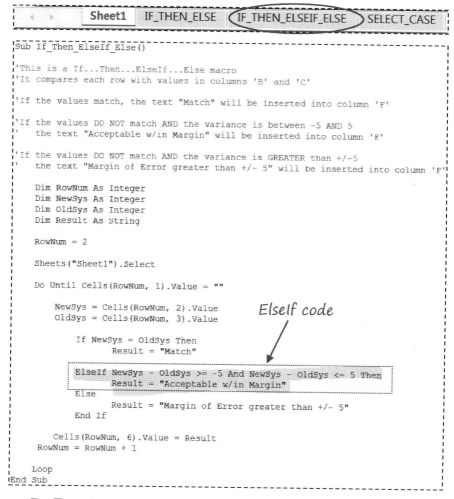

```
Sub If_Then_ElseIf_Else()

'This is a If...Then...ElseIf...Else macro
'It compares each row with values in columns 'B' and 'C'

'If the values match, the text "Match" will be inserted into column 'F'

'If the values DO NOT match AND the variance is between -5 AND 5
'   the text "Acceptable w/in Margin" will be inserted into column 'F'

'If the values DO NOT match AND the variance is GREATER than +/-5
'   the text "Margin of Error greater than +/- 5" will be inserted into column 'F'

    Dim RowNum As Integer
    Dim NewSys As Integer
    Dim OldSys As Integer
    Dim Result As String

    RowNum = 2

    Sheets("Sheet1").Select

    Do Until Cells(RowNum, 1).Value = ""

        NewSys = Cells(RowNum, 2).Value
        OldSys = Cells(RowNum, 3).Value

            If NewSys = OldSys Then
                Result = "Match"

            ElseIf NewSys - OldSys >= -5 And NewSys - OldSys <= 5 Then
                Result = "Acceptable w/in Margin"
            Else
                Result = "Margin of Error greater than +/- 5"
            End If

        Cells(RowNum, 6).Value = Result
    RowNum = RowNum + 1

    Loop
End Sub
```

ElseIf code

7. Test the macro '**If…Then…ElseIf…Else**'

Column 'F' should now have one of the following values:

A. Match
B. Acceptable w/in Margin
C. Margin of Error greater than +/- 5

For our final example, we'll extend our analysis to delineate which records:

A. Are a "System Match 100%"
B. Have a "Variance greater than +/- 5"
C. Acceptable variance "Pass OLD Sys =< 5"
D. Acceptable variance "Pass NEW Sys =< 5"

The required syntax for a **Select...Case** structure:

```
Select Case test expression
      Case [expression list
         [ statements ] ]
      Case Else
         [[ else statements ] ]
   End Select
```

Test expression	Name of the variable being tested (datatype)
Expression list	A true or false value as a result of the test
Statements	Action to be applied for each matching case
Else Statements	Action to be applied for no matching case
End Select	Ends the Select...Case test

FILE FOR EXERCISE:
Chapter12_If_Then_Case_Statements.xlsx

STEPS TO CREATE MACRO (Select...Case)

This **Select...Case** macro cannot be recorded, the code will need to manually entered:

1. Open the file **Chapter12_If_Then_Case_Statements.xlsx**

2. Select the '**Developer**' tab

3. Click the '**Visual Basic**' field

4. Make sure '**Chapter12_If_Then_Case_Statements.xlsx**' is selected (highlighted)

5. From the VBA Editor Ribbon select '**Insert : Module**'

A new module should now be added

6. **Enter** or **copy and paste** the following lines of code from the **'SELECT_CASE'** tab of the spreadsheet into the newly added module:

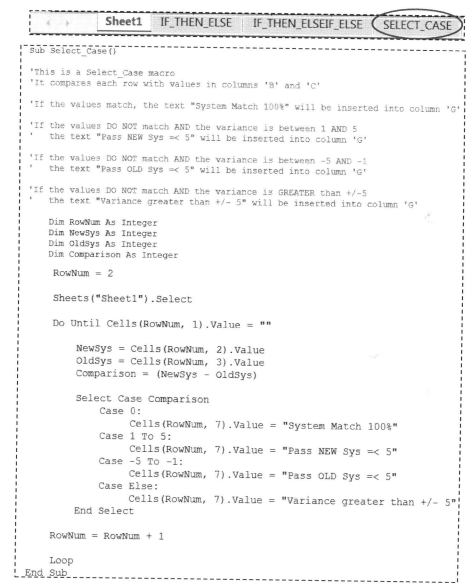

```
Sub Select_Case()

'This is a Select_Case macro
'It compares each row with values in columns 'B' and 'C'

'If the values match, the text "System Match 100%" will be inserted into column 'G'

'If the values DO NOT match AND the variance is between 1 AND 5
'    the text "Pass NEW Sys =< 5" will be inserted into column 'G'

'If the values DO NOT match AND the variance is between -5 AND -1
'    the text "Pass OLD Sys =< 5" will be inserted into column 'G'

'If the values DO NOT match AND the variance is GREATER than +/-5
'    the text "Variance greater than +/- 5" will be inserted into column 'G'

    Dim RowNum As Integer
    Dim NewSys As Integer
    Dim OldSys As Integer
    Dim Comparison As Integer

    RowNum = 2

    Sheets("Sheet1").Select

    Do Until Cells(RowNum, 1).Value = ""

        NewSys = Cells(RowNum, 2).Value
        OldSys = Cells(RowNum, 3).Value
        Comparison = (NewSys - OldSys)

        Select Case Comparison
            Case 0:
                Cells(RowNum, 7).Value = "System Match 100%"
            Case 1 To 5:
                Cells(RowNum, 7).Value = "Pass NEW Sys =< 5"
            Case -5 To -1:
                Cells(RowNum, 7).Value = "Pass OLD Sys =< 5"
            Case Else:
                Cells(RowNum, 7).Value = "Variance greater than +/- 5"
        End Select

    RowNum = RowNum + 1

    Loop
End Sub
```

7. Test the macro '**Select…Case**'

Column 'G' should now have one of the following values:
- A. System Match 100%
- B. Variance greater than +/- 5
- C. Pass OLD Sys =< 5
- D. Pass NEW Sys =< 5

CODE REVIEW (Select...Case)

As you can see conditional evaluation is written more concisely than the If...Then...ElseIf...Else structure, making it simpler to expand comparisons and easier to test and maintain.

```
Sub Select_Case()
            Variables
    Dim RowNum As Integer
    Dim NewSys As Integer
    Dim OldSys As Integer
    Dim Comparison As Integer
                                        Test expression
                                        variable being tested
    RowNum = 2

    Do Until Cells(RowNum, 1).Value = ""

        NewSys = Cells(RowNum, 2).Value
        OldSys = Cells(RowNum, 3).Value
        Comparison = (NewSys - OldSys)
                                            Statements: Action to be
                                            applied if Case value is True
        Select Case Comparison
Expression List     Case 0:
variable being tested =     Cells(RowNum, 7).Value = "System Match 100%"
Case 0 or           Case 1 To 5:
   1 or                 Cells(RowNum, 7).Value = "Pass NEW Sys =< 5"
  -4 or             Case -5 To -1:
   6 etc.               Cells(RowNum, 7).Value = "Pass OLD Sys =< 5"
                    Case Else:
                        Cells(RowNum, 7).Value = "Variance greater than +/- 5"
        End Select

        RowNum = RowNum + 1

    Loop
End Sub
```

CHAPTER 13

Data Analysis Macro #2 – Enhanced comparative analysis

MACRO OBJECTIVES

- To demonstrate how incorporating a **Do...loop** and a **Select...Case decision structure** into a macro can improve data analysis

---

SCENARIO:

You're a QA analyst working on a data migration project. You're responsible for comparing the results between an old and new parts system. You have been informed you may have to complete between 75 – 100 tests and the number of records being tested will fluctuate with each comparison. The following are the requirements for each iteration:

1. Compare the results of the two systems, identify the records with the following labels:
   a. System Match 100%
   b. Pass NEW Sys =< 5
   c. Pass OLD Sys =< 5
   d. Variance greater than +/- 5

2. Highlight with shading the records with a variance greater than +/- 5 between the two systems.
   a. Apply an AutoFilter to allow for easy identification of the records with a variance greater than +/- 5

3. Insert a tab with the following information:
   a. Provides a summary of the results
   b. Identifies the date and time the test was completed

WEB ADDRESS & FILE NAME FOR EXERCISE:
http://bentonexcelbooks.my-free.website/macro-exercise-files
Chapter13_Enhanced_Comparative_Analysis.xlsx

EXAMPLE:

From:

	A	B	C	D
1	**PART #**	**NEW SYSTEM**	**OLD SYSTEM**	
2	Part #1	878	878	
3	Part #2	944	944	
4	Part #3	796	796	
5	Part #4	222	222	
6	Part #5	614	614	
7	Part #6	149	145	
8	Part #7	621	621	
9	Part #8	937	937	
10	Part #9	107	107	
11	Part #10	665	665	
12	Part #11	108	108	
3999	Part #3998	909	909	
4000	Part #3999	689	689	
4001	Part #4000	841	841	

To:

	A	B	C	D
1	**PART #**	**NEW SYSTEM**	**OLD SYSTEM**	**COMPARSION**
2	Part #1	878	878	System Match 100%
3	Part #2	944	944	System Match 100%
4	Part #3	796	805	Variance greater than +/- 5
5	Part #4	222	222	System Match 100%
6	Part #5	614	614	System Match 100%
7	Part #6	149	145	Pass NEW Sys =< 5
8	Part #7	621	621	System Match 100%
9	Part #8	937	937	System Match 100%
10	Part #9	107	110	Pass OLD Sys =< 5

◄ ► | Original | Testing Summary | **Testing Results** | ⊕ | ⋮ | ◄

EXAMPLE Continued.....
TO:

	A	B	C
1	**Testing Summary**		
2	Total number of records	4,000	
3	Records that match 100%	3,979	99.5%
4	Records that pass NEW Sys =< 5	8	0.2%
5	Records that pass OLD Sys =< 5	8	0.2%
6	Records with a variance greater than +/- 5	5	0.1%
7			
8			
9	Testing Completed	3/16/2016 8:40	
10			

| ◄ ► | Original | **Testing Summary** | Testing Results | ⊕ |

STEPS TO CREATE MACRO

This macro utilizes several lessons reviewed in the preceding chapters, it includes portions that are both **recorded** *and* **coded**. To study this macro, you may record the steps outlined in <u>chapter 9</u> or

1. Open the file
   Chapter13_Enhanced_Comparative_Analysis.xlsx

2. Select the '**Developer**' tab

3. Click the **'Visual Basic'** field

4. Make sure
   'Chapter13_Enhanced_Comparative_Analysis.xlsx' is selected (highlighted)

5. From the VBA Editor Ribbon select '**Insert : Module**'

A new module should now be added

6. **Copy and paste** the following lines of code from the '**Macro Code**' tab of the spreadsheet into the newly created module:

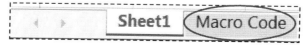

CODE REVIEW

Part 1

```
Sub Enhanced_Comparative_Analysis()

'*********************************************************************
'  PART 1
'*********************************************************************

'Rename 'Sheet1' to 'Original'
    Sheets("Sheet1").Select
    Sheets("Sheet1").Name = "Original"

'Copy newly named 'Original' sheet, name it 'Testing Results'
    Sheets("Original").Select
    Sheets("Original").Copy After:=Sheets(1)
    Sheets("Original (2)").Select
    Sheets("Original (2)").Name = "Testing Results"

'On the newly created 'Testing Results' sheet, label cell 'D1' 'COMPARISON'
    Range("D1").Select
    ActiveCell.FormulaR1C1 = "COMPARSION"
    Range("D1").Select


'*********************************************************************
'  Insert Comparison loop (code must be manually entered)
'*********************************************************************
    Dim RowNum As Integer
    Dim NewSys As Integer
    Dim OldSys As Integer
    Dim Comparison As Integer

    RowNum = 2

    Do Until Cells(RowNum, 1).Value = ""

        NewSys = Cells(RowNum, 2).Value
        OldSys = Cells(RowNum, 3).Value
        Comparison = (NewSys - OldSys)

        Select Case Comparison
            Case 0:
                Cells(RowNum, 4).Value = "System Match 100%"
            Case 1 To 5:
                Cells(RowNum, 4).Value = "Pass NEW Sys =< 5"
            Case -5 To -1:
                Cells(RowNum, 4).Value = "Pass OLD Sys =< 5"
            Case Else:
                Cells(RowNum, 4).Value = "Variance greater than +/- 5"
        End Select

    RowNum = RowNum + 1

    Loop
```

Part 2

```
'*****************************************************************
'   PART 2 (apply conditional formatting and AutoFilter)
'*****************************************************************

'Apply conditional formatting to column 'D'
    Columns("D:D").Select
    Selection.FormatConditions.Add Type:=xlCellValue, Operator:=xlEqual, _
        Formula1:="=""Variance greater than +/- 5"""
    Selection.FormatConditions(Selection.FormatConditions.Count).SetFirstPriority
    With Selection.FormatConditions(1).Font
        .Color = -16383844
        .TintAndShade = 0
    End With
    With Selection.FormatConditions(1).Interior
        .PatternColorIndex = xlAutomatic
        .Color = 13551615
        .TintAndShade = 0
    End With
    Selection.FormatConditions(1).StopIfTrue = False

'Apply AutoFilter to columns 'A:D'
    Range("A1:D1").Select
    Selection.AutoFilter
    Cells.Select
    Cells.EntireColumn.AutoFit
    Range("G13").Select
```

Part 3

```
'*****************************************************************
'   PART 3 (insert new tab, summary count descriptions, & formulas)
'*****************************************************************
'Insert new tab
    Sheets.Add
    ActiveSheet.Name = "Testing Summary"

'Inserting text descriptions into column 'A'
    Range("A1").Select
    ActiveCell.FormulaR1C1 = "Testing Summary"
    Range("A2").Select
    ActiveCell.FormulaR1C1 = "Total number of records"
    Range("A3").Select
    ActiveCell.FormulaR1C1 = "Records that match 100%"
    Range("A4").Select
    ActiveCell.FormulaR1C1 = "Records that pass NEW Sys =< 5"
    Range("A5").Select
     ActiveCell.FormulaR1C1 = "Records that pass OLD Sys =< 5"
    Range("A6").Select
    ActiveCell.FormulaR1C1 = "Records with a variance greater than +/- 5"
    Range("A7").Select
```

Part 3 continued

```
'***********************************************************************
'* PART 3 Inserting CountA and CountIF functions for the Test Summary
'* (code must be manually entered)
'***********************************************************************
    'Total the number of records
    Worksheets("Testing Summary").Cells(2, 2).Value _
    = Application.WorksheetFunction.CountA(Worksheets("Testing Results").Columns("D:D"))

    'Total the number of records that "System Match 100%":
    Worksheets("Testing Summary").Cells(3, 2).Value _
    = Application.WorksheetFunction.CountIf(Worksheets("Testing Results").Columns("D:D"),

    'Total the number of records that  "Pass NEW Sys =< 5":
    Worksheets("Testing Summary").Cells(4, 2).Value _
    = Application.WorksheetFunction.CountIf(Worksheets("Testing Results").Columns("D:D"),

    'Total the number of records that  "Pass OLD Sys =< 5":
    Worksheets("Testing Summary").Cells(5, 2).Value _
    = Application.WorksheetFunction.CountIf(Worksheets("Testing Results").Columns("D:D"),

    'Total the number of records with a "Variance greater than +/- 5":
    Worksheets("Testing Summary").Cells(6, 2).Value _
    = Application.WorksheetFunction.CountIf(Worksheets("Testing Results").Columns("D:D"),
'***********************************************************************

'Changing the width of column 'A'
    Columns("A:A").ColumnWidth = 35

'Inserting % formulas
    Range("C3").Select
    ActiveCell.FormulaR1C1 = "=RC[-1]/R[-1]C[-1]"
    Range("C4").Select
    ActiveCell.FormulaR1C1 = "=RC[-1]/R[-2]C[-1]"
    Range("C5").Select
    ActiveCell.FormulaR1C1 = "=RC[-1]/R[-3]C[-1]"
    Range("C6").Select
    ActiveCell.FormulaR1C1 = "=RC[-1]/R[-4]C[-1]"
```

Part 3 continued

```
'Change the formatting for cells 'C3:C6' to a percent w/ one decimal point
    Range("C3:C6").Select
    Selection.Style = "Percent"
    Selection.NumberFormat = "0.0%"
    Selection.NumberFormat = "0.00%"
    Selection.NumberFormat = "0.0%"

'Change the formatting for cells 'B2:B6' to a number zero decimal point
    Range("B2:B6").Select
    Selection.Style = "Comma"
    Selection.NumberFormat = "_(* #,##0.0_);_(* (#,##0.0);_(* ""-""??_);_(@_)"
    Selection.NumberFormat = "_(* #,##0_);_(* (#,##0);_(* ""-""??_);_(@_)"

'Bold and merge center across columns 'A1:C1'
    Range("A1:C1").Select
    Selection.Font.Bold = True
    With Selection
        .HorizontalAlignment = xlCenter
        .VerticalAlignment = xlBottom
        .WrapText = False
        .Orientation = 0
        .AddIndent = False
        .IndentLevel = 0
        .ShrinkToFit = False
        .ReadingOrder = xlContext
        .MergeCells = False
    End With
    Selection.Merge

'Cell 'A9' add text 'Testing Completed'
    Range("A9").Select
    ActiveCell.FormulaR1C1 = "Testing Completed"

'Cell 'B9' add formula =NOW()
    Range("B9").Select
    ActiveCell.FormulaR1C1 = "=NOW()"
```

```
'Cell 'B9' copy and paste as a value
    Range("B9").Select
    Selection.Copy
    Selection.PasteSpecial Paste:=xlPasteValues, Operation:=xlNone, SkipBlanks _
        :=False, Transpose:=False
    Application.CutCopyMode = False

'Changing the width of column 'B'
    Columns("B:B").ColumnWidth = 14

    Range("A10").Select

End Sub
```

CHAPTER 14
Report macro #2 – Dynamic Quarterly & Year-To-Date reporting

Some sections of this macro are considered advanced and use syntax not covered in earlier chapters. It is intended for readers who have practiced the previous lessons and feel comfortable enough with the VBA language to challenge themselves with an example that illustrates variable reporting.

MACRO OBJECTIVES

- To demonstrate how incorporating multiple **Do…loops** and an **If…Then decision structure** into a macro can create dynamic quarterly and Year-To-Date (YTD) reporting.

SCENARIO:

As a Business Analyst you produce a sales summary report each month, sometimes mid-month upon request. You have access to a database and can generate an Excel® file on-demand that contains sales by month for each location. However, the file <u>does not</u> include *sub-totals by quarter* nor *a YTD total*. You must manually add those columns along with applying formatting each time you produce the report.

You've submitted a request to your IT (Information Technology) Department for these enhancements, but have been told there is a backlog and it could take one year or more to complete your submission.

Since this report is a popular request, you have determined it is worth the time and effort to develop a macro that will produce this report in a matter of seconds. The following are the requirements for each report:

1. Insert a YTD to column, summing all months
2. Insert a quarterly column and sum each three month period
3. Insert a total row, summing all months, quarters, and YTD
4. Insert the report title **'CURRENT SALES BY STORE'**
5. Insert the **'Report created on <date>:'** as the report may be generated mid-month

WEB ADDRESS & FILE NAME FOR EXERCISE:
http://bentonexcelbooks.my-free.website/macro-exercise-files
Chapter14_Quarterly_YTD_reporting.xlsx

EXAMPLE:
From:

LOCATION #	Jan	Feb	Mar	Apr	May	Jun
Store #1	406	184	343	134	320	498
Store #2	332	260	470	161	485	305
Store #3	496	124	427	396	194	241
Store #4	152	442	360	259	457	184
Store #5	178	241	431	314	311	114
Store #6	371	183	198	167	431	366
Store #7	172	116	422	343	250	337
Store #8	173	252	247	278	226	364
Store #9	405	127	221	250	220	328
Store #10	205	178	245	249	249	467
Store #11	494	107	222	496	246	433
Store #12	472	116	174	387	183	107
Store #13	491	162	115	329	166	437
Store #14	267	315	139	372	386	286
Store #15	201	451	389	210	152	165

| Jan-Feb | Q1 | Q2 | Q3 | Q4 | (+) |

To:

CURRENT SALES BY STORE

Report created on: 02/Jul/2016

LOCATION #	Jan	Feb	Mar	QTR 1	Apr	May	Jun	QTR 2	YTD
Store #1	406	184	343	$ 933	134	320	498	$ 952	$ 1,885
Store #2	332	260	470	$ 1,062	161	485	305	$ 951	$ 2,013
Store #3	496	124	427	$ 1,047	396	194	241	$ 831	$ 1,878
Store #4	152	442	360	$ 954	259	457	184	$ 900	$ 1,854
Store #5	178	241	431	$ 850	314	311	114	$ 739	$ 1,589
Store #6	371	183	198	$ 752	167	431	366	$ 964	$ 1,716
Store #7	172	116	422	$ 710	343	250	337	$ 930	$ 1,640
Store #8	173	252	247	$ 672	278	226	364	$ 868	$ 1,540
Store #9	405	127	221	$ 753	250	220	328	$ 798	$ 1,551
Store #10	205	178	245	$ 628	249	249	467	$ 965	$ 1,593
Store #11	494	107	222	$ 823	496	246	433	$ 1,175	$ 1,998
Store #12	472	116	174	$ 762	387	183	107	$ 677	$ 1,439
Store #13	491	162	115	$ 768	329	166	437	$ 932	$ 1,700
Store #14	267	315	139	$ 721	372	386	286	$ 1,044	$ 1,765
Store #15	201	451	389	$ 1,041	210	152	165	$ 527	$ 1,568
TOTAL	$ 4,815	$ 3,258	$ 4,403	$ 12,476	$ 4,345	$ 4,276	$ 4,632	$ 13,253	$ 25,729

STEPS TO CREATE MACRO

This macro utilizes several lessons reviewed in the preceding chapters, it includes portions that are both **recorded** *and* **coded**. To study this macro, it is easiest to copy and paste the code from the **'Macro Code' tab** of the spreadsheet named **'Chapter14_Quarterly_YTD_reporting.xlsx'** into a newly created module.

IMPORTANT!

This macro will create the report based on the data in the selected tab. Therefore, it is important to only launch this macro when one of the following tabs is selected:
1. Jan-Feb
2. Q1 *or* Q2 *or* Q3 *or* Q4
DO NOT run from the 'Macro Code' worksheet.

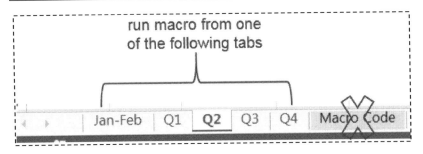

CODE REVIEW
Part 1

```
Sub QTR_YTD_Reporting()

    Dim LastCol As Long
    Dim RowNum As Integer
    Dim ColNum As Integer
    Dim CurrentQtr As Integer
    Dim CurrentCellValue As String
    Dim LastRow As Long

'************************************************************************
'Identifies the last column with data in the worksheet and
'then inserts a new column and labels it 'YTD'
'************************************************************************
    LastCol = ActiveSheet.UsedRange.Columns(ActiveSheet.UsedRange.Columns.Count).Column + 1
    Cells(1, LastCol).EntireColumn.Insert
    Cells(1, LastCol).Value = "YTD"

        'Formats YTD column header
        '---------------Begin formatting---------------
        Cells(1, LastCol).Select
        'This section was recorded to obtain correct formatting syntax and then
        'copied and pasted below
        Selection.Font.Bold = True
        With Selection.Interior
            .Pattern = xlSolid
            .PatternColorIndex = xlAutomatic
            .ThemeColor = xlThemeColorDark2
            .TintAndShade = -9.99786370433668E-02
            .PatternTintAndShade = 0
        End With
        '-----------End formatting-----------
```

```
'************************************************************************
'Loop #1 (Do...Until)
'Loops through each row and sums all columns to determine the YTD totals for each store#
'************************************************************************
    RowNum = 2

    Do Until Cells(RowNum, 1) = ""
        Cells(RowNum, LastCol).Value = WorksheetFunction.Sum(Range(Cells(RowNum, 2), _
                                Cells(RowNum, LastCol - 1)))
        'Formats YTD column rows
        '---------------Begin formatting---------------
        Cells(RowNum, LastCol).Select
        'This section was recorded to obtain correct formatting syntax and then
        'copied and pasted below
            Selection.Font.Bold = True
        With Selection.Interior
            .Pattern = xlSolid
            .PatternColorIndex = xlAutomatic
            .ThemeColor = xlThemeColorDark2
            .TintAndShade = -9.99786370433668E-02
            .PatternTintAndShade = 0
        End With
            Selection.Style = "Currency"
            Selection.NumberFormat = "_($* #,##0.0_);_($* (#,##0.0);_($* ""-""??_);_(@_)"
            Selection.NumberFormat = "_($* #,##0_);_($* (#,##0);_($* ""-""??_);_(@_)"
        '---------------End formatting---------------

    RowNum = RowNum + 1
    Loop
```

```
'********************************************************************
'Loop #2 (Do...While) with If...Then decision structure to determine QTR columns
'Loop #3 (Do...Until) sums the 3 months for each QTR
'********************************************************************
    CurrentQtr = 1
    ColNum = 2

    Do While ColNum <= ActiveSheet.UsedRange.Columns(ActiveSheet.UsedRange.Columns.Count).Column
            CurrentCellValue = Cells(1, ColNum).Value

    ---> Nested inside Loop #2    ***If...Then decision structure to determine QTR columns***
            If CurrentCellValue = "Mar" Or CurrentCellValue = "Jun" Or _
            CurrentCellValue = "Sep" Or CurrentCellValue = "Dec" Then
                    Cells(1, ColNum + 1).EntireColumn.Insert
                    Cells(1, ColNum + 1).Value = "QTR " & CurrentQtr
                    CurrentQtr = CurrentQtr + 1

                    'Formats the QTR column header
                    '------------Begin formatting------------
                    Cells(1, ColNum + 1).Select
                    'This section was recorded to obtain correct formatting syntax and then
                    'copied and pasted below
                            Selection.Font.Bold = True
                        With Selection.Interior
                            .Pattern = xlSolid
                            .PatternColorIndex = xlAutomatic
                            .ThemeColor = xlThemeColorAccent1
                            .TintAndShade = 0.799981688894314
                            .PatternTintAndShade = 0
                        End With
                            Selection.Style = "Currency"
                            Selection.NumberFormat = "_($* #,##0.0_);_($* (#,##0.0);_($* ""-""
                            Selection.NumberFormat = "_($* #,##0_);_($* (#,##0);_($* ""-""??_)
                    '------------End formatting------------
```

```
    ---> Nested inside Loop #2    ***Loop #3 (Do...Until) sums the 3 months for each QTR***
                    RowNum = 2

                    Do Until Cells(RowNum, 1) = ""
                            Cells(RowNum, ColNum + 1).Value = _
                            WorksheetFunction.Sum(Range(Cells(RowNum, ColNum - 2), Cells(RowNum, ColNum)))

                    'Formats each QTR row
                    '------------Begin formatting------------
                    Cells(RowNum, ColNum + 1).Select
                    'This section was recorded to obtain correct formatting syntax and then
                    'copied and pasted below
                            Selection.Font.Bold = True
                    With Selection.Interior
                            .Pattern = xlSolid
                            .PatternColorIndex = xlAutomatic
                            .ThemeColor = xlThemeColorAccent1
                            .TintAndShade = 0.799981688894314
                            .PatternTintAndShade = 0
                    End With
                            Selection.Style = "Currency"
                            Selection.NumberFormat = "_($* #,##0.0_);_($* (#,##0.0);_($* ""-""??_);_(@_)"
                            Selection.NumberFormat = "_($* #,##0_);_($* (#,##0);_($* ""-""??_);_(@_)"
                    '------------End formatting------------

                    RowNum = RowNum + 1

                    Loop
                    ------------------------------

            End If

    ColNum = ColNum + 1

    Loop
```

```
'********************************************************************************
'Identifies the last row with data in the worksheet and inserts the label 'TOTAL' into column 'A'
'of the next blank row
'********************************************************************************
    LastRow = ActiveSheet.UsedRange.Rows(ActiveSheet.UsedRange.Rows.Count).Row

    Cells(LastRow, 1).Offset(1, 0).Select
    Cells(LastRow, 1).Offset(1, 0).Value = "TOTAL"

        'Formats the 'TOTAL' label in column 'A'
        '-----------Begin formatting-----------
        Cells(LastRow, 1).Offset(1, 0).Select
        'This section was recorded to obtain correct formatting syntax and then
        'copied and pasted below
        Selection.Font.Bold = True
        With Selection.Interior
            .Pattern = xlSolid
            .PatternColorIndex = xlAutomatic
            .ThemeColor = xlThemeColorDark2
            .TintAndShade = -9.99786370433668E-02
            .PatternTintAndShade = 0
        End With
        '-----------End formatting-----------
```

```
'********************************************************************************
'Loop #4 (Do...Until) sums each column...Month, QTR, & YTD
'********************************************************************************
        CurrentColumn = 2
        LastColumn = ActiveSheet.UsedRange.Columns(ActiveSheet.UsedRange.Columns.Count).Column

        Do Until CurrentColumn > LastColumn

            Cells(LastRow + 1, CurrentColumn).Value = _
            WorksheetFunction.Sum(Range(Cells(2, CurrentColumn), Cells(LastRow, CurrentColumn)))
            Cells(LastRow, 1).Offset(1, 0).Select

            CurrentColumn = CurrentColumn + 1

        'Formats each TOTAL row for Month, QTR, & YTD
        '-----------Begin formatting-----------
        Cells(LastRow, CurrentColumn - 1).Offset(1, 0).Select
        'This section was recorded to obtain correct formatting syntax and then
        'copied and pasted below
        Selection.Font.Bold = True
        With Selection.Interior
            .Pattern = xlSolid
            .PatternColorIndex = xlAutomatic
            .ThemeColor = xlThemeColorDark2
            .TintAndShade = -9.99786370433668E-02
            .PatternTintAndShade = 0
        End With
        Selection.Style = "Currency"
        Selection.NumberFormat = "_($* #,##0.0_);_($* (#,##0.0);_($* ""-""??_);_(@_)"
        Selection.NumberFormat = "_($* #,##0_);_($* (#,##0);_($* ""-""??_);_(@_)"
        '-----------End formatting-----------

        Loop
```

```
'*****************************************************************************
'Additional report formatting (Report Title & Date)
'The below section was recorded to obtain the correct formatting syntax and then copied and pasted
'*****************************************************************************
    Rows("1:1").Select
    Selection.Insert Shift:=xlDown, CopyOrigin:=xlFormatFromLeftOrAbove

    Range("A1").Select
    ActiveCell.FormulaR1C1 = "CURRENT SALES BY STORE"

    Rows("2:2").Select
    Selection.Insert Shift:=xlDown, CopyOrigin:=xlFormatFromLeftOrAbove

    Range("A2").Select
    ActiveCell.FormulaR1C1 = "Report created on:"

    Range("C2").Select
    ActiveCell.FormulaR1C1 = "=NOW()"
    Range("C2").Select
    Selection.NumberFormat = "dd/mmm/yyyy"
    Range("C2").Select
    Selection.Copy
    Selection.PasteSpecial Paste:=xlPasteValues, Operation:=xlNone, SkipBlanks _
        :=False, Transpose:=False
    Application.CutCopyMode = False
    Columns("C:C").Select
    Selection.ColumnWidth = 12
```

```
    Rows("3:3").Select
    Selection.Insert Shift:=xlDown, CopyOrigin:=xlFormatFromLeftOrAbove

    Range("A1").Select
    Selection.Font.Bold = True
    With Selection.Font
        .Name = "Arial"
        .Size = 18
        .Strikethrough = False
        .Superscript = False
        .Subscript = False
        .OutlineFont = False
        .Shadow = False
        .Underline = xlUnderlineStyleNone
        .ThemeColor = xlThemeColorLight1
        .TintAndShade = 0
        .ThemeFont = xlThemeFontNone
    End With
    Range("A3").Select

End Sub
```

CHAPTER 15

Macro to print all worksheets in a workbook

MACRO OBJECTIVES

- Use a macro to print all worksheets in a workbook

STEPS TO CREATE MACRO

This macro cannot be recorded, the code will need to be manually entered. Since this macro can be used with multiple workbooks it is suggested to add to the **Personal Macro Workbook** *(The 'PERSONAL.XLSB' macro workbook is hidden by default)*, please see chapter 5 if you're unfamiliar with how this file works:

1. Create a new blank Excel® spreadsheet **(CTRL + N)**
2. Select the '**Developer**' tab
3. Click the **'Visual Basic'** field

The VBA Editor will open:

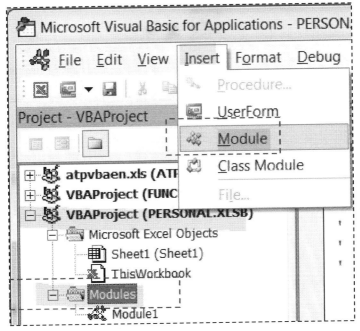

4. Make sure **'PERSONAL.XLSB'** is selected (highlighted)

5. From the VBA Editor Ribbon select **'Insert : Module'**

A new module should now be added

6. Add the following lines of code:

```
Sub Print_All_Tabs()

' This macro will print all worksheet tabs

    ActiveWorkbook.Worksheets.PrintOut _
    Copies:=1
' You may adjust the number of copies

End Sub
```

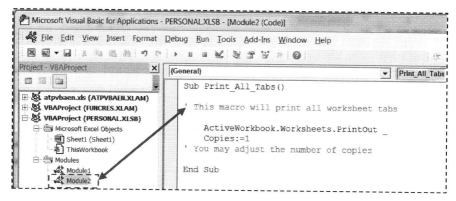

7. Click the **'Save'** button or **'CTRL+S'** from the **VBA Editor** to save the coding changes to the **'PERSONAL.XLSB'** macro workbook

8. Test macro on a workbook that has multiple worksheets to print

9. If unhidden, **hide** the **'PERSONAL.XLSB'** macro workbook *(from the Ribbon select 'VIEW : Hide')*

10. When exiting Excel®, click the **'Save'** button when prompted to save the changes to the '**Personal Macro Workbook**'

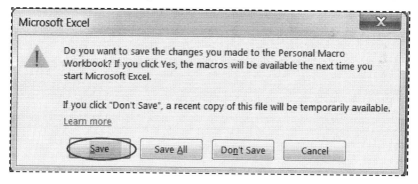

CHAPTER 16

Macro to save each worksheet as a separate workbook files

MACRO OBJECTIVES
- Use a macro to save all worksheets as separate workbooks

WEB ADDRESS & FILE NAME FOR EXERCISE:
http://bentonexcelbooks.my-free.website/macro-exercise-files
Chapter16_Save_Each_Worksheet.xlsx

STEPS TO CREATE MACRO

This macro cannot be recorded, the code will need to be manually entered. We will be using a 'For Each...Next' loop, since this macro can be used with multiple workbooks it is suggested to add to the **Personal Macro Workbook** *(The 'PERSONAL.XLSB' macro workbook is hidden by default)*, please see chapter 5 if you're unfamiliar with how this file works:

1. If you have not already done so, please create a folder to save the files to. This example uses the file path: **'C:\MacroTrainingBook\'**
2. Open the file **'Chapter16_Save_Each_Worksheet.xlsx'**
3. Select the '**Developer**' tab
4. Click the **'Visual Basic'** field

The VBA Editor will open

5. Make sure **'PERSONAL.XLSB'** is selected (highlighted)
6. From the VBA Editor Ribbon select **'Insert : Module'**

A new module should now be added

7. **Enter** or **Copy and paste** the following lines of code from the **'Macro Code'** tab of the spreadsheet into the newly created module:

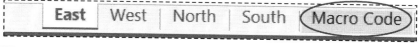

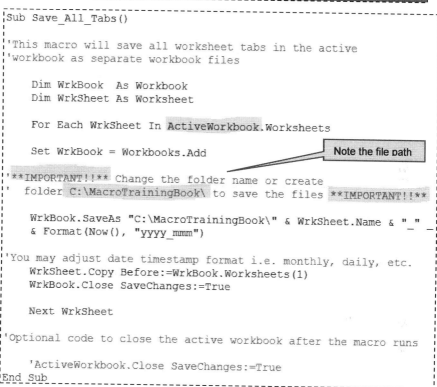

```
Sub Save_All_Tabs()

'This macro will save all worksheet tabs in the active
'workbook as separate workbook files

    Dim WrkBook  As Workbook
    Dim WrkSheet As Worksheet

    For Each WrkSheet In ActiveWorkbook.Worksheets

    Set WrkBook = Workbooks.Add

'**IMPORTANT!!** Change the folder name or create
'  folder C:\MacroTrainingBook\ to save the files **IMPORTANT!!**

    WrkBook.SaveAs "C:\MacroTrainingBook\" & WrkSheet.Name & "_"
    & Format(Now(), "yyyy_mmm")

'You may adjust date timestamp format i.e. monthly, daily, etc.
    WrkSheet.Copy Before:=WrkBook.Worksheets(1)
    WrkBook.Close SaveChanges:=True

    Next WrkSheet

'Optional code to close the active workbook after the macro runs

    'ActiveWorkbook.Close SaveChanges:=True
End Sub
```

Note the file path

8. Click the **'Save'** button or **'CTRL+S'** from the **VBA Editor** to save the coding changes to the **'PERSONAL.XLSB'** macro workbook

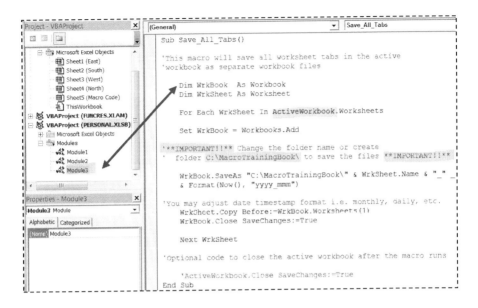

9. Test macro

You should get results *similar* to the below screenshot:

Name	Date modified
Chapter10	4/14/2016 11:06 A...
East_2016_Apr.xlsx	4/7/2016 8:28 AM
Macro Code_2016_Apr.xlsx	4/7/2016 8:28 AM
North_2016_Apr.xlsx	4/7/2016 8:28 AM
South_2016_Apr.xlsx	4/7/2016 8:28 AM
West_2016_Apr.xlsx	4/7/2016 8:28 AM

10. If unhidden, **hide** the **'PERSONAL.XLSB'** macro workbook *(from the Ribbon select 'VIEW : Hide')*

11. When exiting Excel®, click the **'Save'** button when prompted to save the changes to the '**Personal Macro Workbook'**

CHAPTER 17

Macros to sort worksheets either alphabetically or numerically

---

MACRO OBJECTIVES

- Use a macro to sort worksheets alphabetically
- Use a macro to sort worksheets numerically

SCENARIO:

You produce two reports each month, one by sales person and the other by location number. To save time and provide a simpler viewing experience for your customers, you create the following two macros:

1. A macro to sort tabs in alphabetical order by sales person *last name*

2. A macro to sort tabs in numeric order by *location number*

WEB ADDRESS & FILE NAME FOR EXERCISE:
http://bentonexcelbooks.my-free.website/macro-exercise-files
Chapter17_Tab_Sorting_**Alphabetically**.xlsx
Chapter17_Tab_Sorting_**Numerically**.xlsx

Sorting worksheets alphabetically:

EXAMPLE:
From (non-alphabetical):

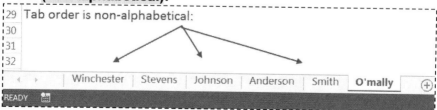

149

To (alphabetical):

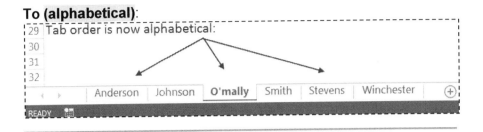

STEPS TO CREATE MACRO

This macro cannot be recorded, the code will need to be manually entered. Since this macro can be used with multiple workbooks it is suggested to add to the **Personal Macro Workbook** *(The 'PERSONAL.XLSB' macro workbook is hidden by default)*, please see chapter 5 if you're unfamiliar with how this file works:

1. Open the file **'Chapter17_Tab_Sorting_Alphabetically.xlsx'**
2. Select the '**Developer**' tab
3. Click the **'Visual Basic'** field

The VBA Editor will open

4. Make sure **'PERSONAL.XLSB'** is selected (highlighted)
5. From the VBA Editor Ribbon select **'Insert : Module'**

A new module should now be added

6. **Enter** or **Copy and paste** the following lines of code from the **'Macro Code'** tab of the spreadsheet into the newly created module:

```
Sub SortTabsAlphabetically()
'This macro will sort text tabs alphabetically
'
        Dim NumberOfSheets As Integer
        Dim Alpha1 As Integer
        Dim Alpha2 As Integer

        NumberOfSheets = Worksheets.Count

        If NumberOfSheets = 1 Then Exit Sub

        For Alpha1 = 1 To NumberOfSheets - 1
        For Alpha2 = Alpha1 + 1 To NumberOfSheets

        If Worksheets(Alpha2).Name < Worksheets(Alpha1).Name _
        Then
            Worksheets(Alpha2).Move before:=Worksheets(Alpha1)
        End If

        Next Alpha2
        Next Alpha1
End Sub
```

7. Test the macro

Sorting worksheets numerically:

EXAMPLE:
From:

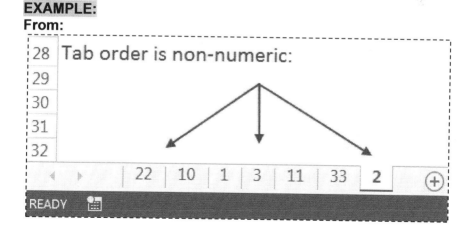

To:

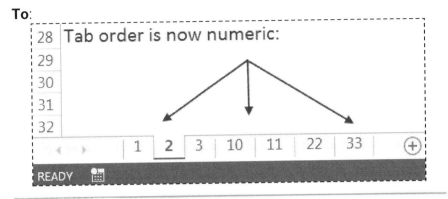

1. Open the file '**Chapter17_Tab_Sorting_Numerically.xlsx**'

2. Select the '**Developer**' tab

3. Click the '**Visual Basic**' field

The VBA Editor will open

4. Make sure '**PERSONAL.XLSB**' is selected (highlighted)

5. From the VBA Editor Ribbon select '**Insert : Module**'

A new module should now be added

6. **Enter** or **Copy and paste** the following lines of code from the '**Macro Code**' tab of the spreadsheet into the newly created module:

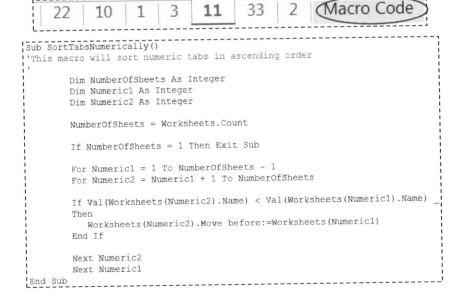

```
Sub SortTabsNumerically()
'This macro will sort numeric tabs in ascending order

        Dim NumberOfSheets As Integer
        Dim Numeric1 As Integer
        Dim Numeric2 As Integer

        NumberOfSheets = Worksheets.Count

        If NumberOfSheets = 1 Then Exit Sub

        For Numeric1 = 1 To NumberOfSheets - 1
        For Numeric2 = Numeric1 + 1 To NumberOfSheets

        If Val(Worksheets(Numeric2).Name) < Val(Worksheets(Numeric1).Name)
        Then
            Worksheets(Numeric2).Move before:=Worksheets(Numeric1)
        End If

        Next Numeric2
        Next Numeric1
End Sub
```

1. Test the macro

2. Click the **'Save'** button or **'CTRL+S'** from the **VBA Editor** to save the coding changes to the **'PERSONAL.XLSB'** macro workbook

3. If unhidden, **hide** the **'PERSONAL.XLSB'** macro workbook *(from the Ribbon select 'VIEW : Hide')*

4. When exiting Excel®, click the **'Save'** button when prompted to save the changes to the '**Personal Macro Workbook'**

CHAPTER 18

Protecting macro code

There may be times when you want to prevent others from being able to modify and view your VBA code. To block users from accessing this information:

1. Open the VBA Editor
2. Select the module you would like to protect
3. From the toolbar select **Tools : VBAProject Properties**

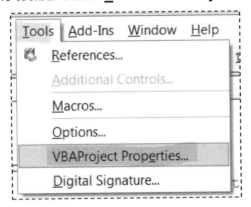

4. When the prompt **VBAProject Properties** appears, select the **'Protection'** tab
5. Click the **'Lock project for viewing'** checkbox
6. Enter a password
7. Click the **'OK'** button

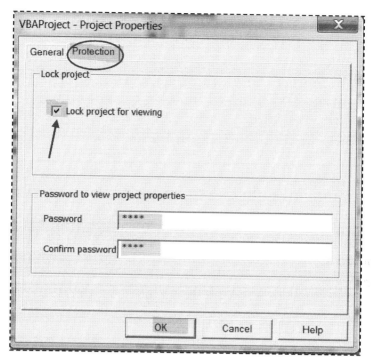

8. Close the VBA Editor

9. **Save** & **Close** the workbook with the now protected macro *(you must save, close, and reopen the workbook for the changes to go into effect)*

10. Reopen the workbook with the protected macro

If someone attempts to view the code with the protected macro, they'll receive the following prompt:

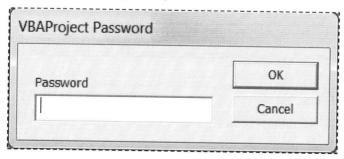

Appendix A

Document Inspector

Occasionally when saving Excel® macro files you'll receive the following message:

Be careful! Parts of your document may include personal information that can't be removed by the Document Inspector.

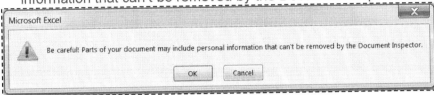

This is caused because Microsoft® does not support the automatic removal of hidden information for documents that use Information Rights Management (IRM). To learn more please visit the following **Microsoft® websites**:

https://support.office.com/en-us/article/Remove-hidden-data-and-personal-information-by-inspecting-workbooks-fdcb68f4-b6e1-4e92-9872-686cc64b6949

https://blogs.office.com/2014/12/09/new-document-inspector-features-excel-powerpoint-word/#4BqYXAW1AakrRRLz.97

https://msdn.microsoft.com/en-us/library/office/ff862071.aspx

HOW TO USE 'DOCUMENT INSPECTOR':

1. To launch **'Document Inspector'**, select the '**File**' menu

2. Form the '**Info**' screen click the drop-down for **'Check for Issues'** and select **'Inspect Document'**

3. Click the **'Inspect'** button

You'll notice the **Macros, Forms, and ActiveX Controls warning**

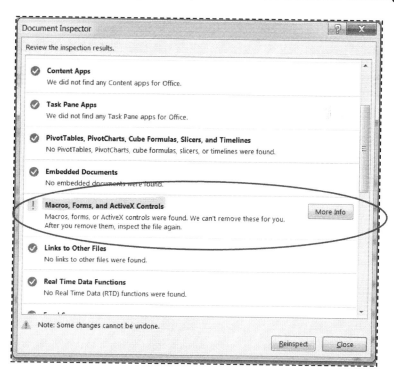

A MESSAGE FROM THE AUTHOR

Thank you!

Thank you for purchasing and reading this book, I hope you found it helpful! Your feedback is valued and appreciated! Please take a few minutes and leave a review.

OTHER BOOKS AVAILABLE FROM THIS AUTHOR

1. Microsoft® Excel® **Start Here** The Beginners Guide

2. The Step-By-Step Guide To The **25 Most Common** Microsoft® Excel® Formulas & Features

3. The Step-By-Step Guide To **Pivot Tables &** Introduction To **Dashboards**

4. The Step-By-Step Guide To The **VLOOKUP** formula in Microsoft® Excel®

5. The Microsoft® Excel® Step-By-Step Training Guide **Book Bundle**

38300925R00095

Made in the USA
Middletown, DE
16 December 2016